2000

Study Strategies
for Lifelong Learning

Series Titles

*Becoming Reflective Students and Teachers With Portfolios
  and Authentic Assessment*—Paris & Ayres

Creating Culturally Responsive Classrooms—Shade, Kelly, & Oberg

*Creating Responsible Learners: The Role of a Positive Classroom
  Environment*—Ridley & Walther

Developing Self-Regulated Learners: Beyond Achievement to Self-Efficacy—
  Zimmerman, Bonner, & Kovach

Inventive Strategies for Teaching Mathematics—Middleton & Goepfert

Motivating Hard to Reach Students—McCombs & Pope

*New Approaches to Literacy: Helping Students Develop Reading
  and Writing Skills*—Marzano & Paynter

*Overcoming Student Failure: Changing Motives and Incentives
  for Learning*—Covington & Teel

Real-Life Problem Solving: A Collaborative Approach to Interdisciplinary Learning—Jones,
  Rasmussen, & Moffitt

Study Strategies for Lifelong Learning—Weinstein & Hume

Teaching for Thinking—Sternberg & Spear–Swerling

Study Strategies
for Lifelong Learning

Claire Ellen Weinstein and Laura M. Hume

AMERICAN PSYCHOLOGICAL ASSOCIATION | WASHINGTON, DC

Published by
American Psychological Association
750 First Street, NE
Washington, DC 20002-4242

Copies may be ordered from
APA Order Department
P.O. Box 92984
Washington, DC 20090-2984

In the UK and Europe, copies may be ordered from
American Psychological Association
3 Henrietta Street
Covent Garden, London
WC2E 8LU England

Typeset in Berkeley and Arbitrary by Monotype Composition,
    Baltimore, MD
Printer: Data Reproductions Corp., Auburn Hills, MI
Cover Designer: Minker Design, Bethesda, MD
Technical/Production Editor: Sarah J. Trembath

Library of Congress Cataloging-in-Publication Data
Weinstein, Claire E.
    Study strategies for lifelong learning / by Claire Ellen Weinstein
and Laura M. Hume.
        p.   cm. — (Psychology in the classroom)
    Includes bibliographical references (p.   ).
    ISBN 1-55798-499-9 (alk. paper)
    1. Study skills.   2. Learning.   3. School children.   I. Hume,
Laura M.   II. Title.   III. Series.
LB1601.W42   1998
371.3'028'1—dc21   98-11396
                                                                CIP

British Library Cataloguing-in-Publication Data
A CIP record is available from the British Library.

Printed in the United States of America
First Edition

	CONTENTS

vii	Preface

1	Introduction
	Student Example: Juliet
	Student Example: Ramon
	Overview of the Book
	Statement of Rationale and Goals

9	Goal 1: Defining Strategic Learning
	What is a Strategic Learner?
	The Skill Domain
	Suggested Readings

23	Goal 2: Understanding the Categories and Characteristics of Learning Strategies
	Rehearsal Strategies for Basic Learning Tasks
	Rehearsal Strategies for Complex Learning Tasks
	Elaboration Strategies for Basic Learning Tasks
	Elaboration Strategies for Complex Learning Tasks
	Organizational Strategies for Basic Learning Tasks
	Organizational Strategies for Complex Learning Tasks
	Declarative, Procedural, and Conditional Knowledge About Strategies
	Pre-, During-, & Posttask Strategies
	Suggested Readings

43	Goal 3: Understanding How to Teach Learning and Study Strategies
	Three Categories of Teaching Methods
	Helping Students Approach Learning Systematically
	Facilitating Student Awareness of the Five Types of Knowledge
	Suggested Readings

71	Goal 4: Helping Students Develop a Repertoire of Strategies
	Assessing Students' Learning Strategies
	A Systematic Approach to Learning
	Strategic Planning: A Project to Facilitate Systematic Strategy Use
	Other Related Variables That Will Affect the Learning and Performance Outcomes
	Checking Back With Juliet and Ramon
	Suggested Readings

95 Final Review

            Outline of Key Ideas

101 Glossary

105 References

111 About the Authors

PREFACE

Effective teaching requires students to play an active role in their own learning. If students do not know how to use a variety of study and learning strategies, it will be hard for them to benefit from instruction, no matter how well the instruction is planned or implemented. Learning can become frustrating for the student and the teacher. This book was written to share with you—the elementary and middle school teacher—a perspective and approach for helping your students play a more active role in their studying and learning.

The ideas, information, and guidelines in this book are based on current models of student learning developed by educational psychologists and the research associated with these models, the evaluation of programs and projects designed to increase student learning, and input from teachers like yourself. There are many things you can do that will help your students to become better, more independent learners who can share much of the responsibility for their own learning. The approaches and activities that we present will give you the tools you need to help your students on their way to becoming effective lifelong learners.

This book is designed to engage you in ways of thinking and in activities that will support and enhance your role as a classroom teacher, as well as providing sample activities you can use with your students. More specifically, it is designed to build on your existing knowledge, experience, and skill in helping students to learn how to study, transform information into knowledge, and develop a systematic approach to learning.

introduction

As teachers, we are constantly working with students who have difficulty studying and learning. Some of the student difficulties teachers encounter are due to physical or psychological problems, but most difficulties are due to problems students have with their knowledge of or skills in learning and study strategies. Take a few minutes and go over the two examples that follow. Think about (a) the learning and study difficulties exhibited by each of these students, (b) how you would try to help each of them, and (c) why you think these would be useful approaches or methods.

| **STUDENT EXAMPLE: JULIET** | Juliet is a third-grade student in a rural school. She is a pleasant, hardworking girl who has many |

friends. Juliet's teacher is concerned because Juliet is having difficulties reading. The problem is appearing just as Juliet is required to read more extensive stories. She understands the words individually; however, she seems to get lost quickly and lose the thread of the plot. When her teacher asks her the meaning of a single sentence, Juliet is generally able to paraphrase it, but she seems unable to do this for an entire story. This problem seems to get worse when Juliet is asked to read aloud. Although she is able to read each word individually, if she is asked to explain what she just read, she is unable to do so. Juliet's teacher often has her students read aloud to begin the stories and then read silently at their desks and answer questions pertaining to the stories. Juliet tries to comply, but she gets frustrated when she has to answer the questions. After she has read the story, she reads a question and appears to hunt for the answer sentence by sentence. Juliet, who has always been a good student, is beginning to get frustrated. Her grades on her reading homework are lower than she has ever made, and she appears to be losing confidence in her ability to improve. Juliet's teacher has talked to her parents, and although they are sympathetic and try to encourage Juliet to do her homework, they don't know how to help her without actually doing the homework for her. Because Juliet takes so long and has so much trouble with reading-comprehension tasks, she is beginning to lose interest in any class work that involves reading. Her teacher knows that Juliet is bright and capable and that tests for a reading disability have not revealed any problems. Her teacher knows that she needs to intervene now, before Juliet's difficulties with reading seriously affect her self-confidence and enthusiasm for school.

1 What, if any, learning and study difficulties are exhibited by Juliet?

2 What would you do to try to help her with these difficulties?

3 Why do you think these would be useful approaches or methods?

STUDENT EXAMPLE: RAMON Ramon is a sixth-grade student at a suburban middle school. The school he moved from in the fourth grade was an inner-city school in another state with a different curriculum. He is well liked by his classmates and his teachers. Ramon pays attention in class and completes all of his homework assignments. His math and science teachers are concerned, however, because he is not doing as well as they think he should be doing. He has great difficulties with tests in almost all of his classes. He claims that he has read all of the material and done all of the homework. His homeroom teacher talked to his parents, and they said that he studies hard at home. On tests days, he can often be heard telling his friends how many hours he studied and how well he knows the material, but his performance does not show the efforts he put in. This is particularly true in his math and science classes. Ramon doesn't seem to understand why he isn't doing better. He says that he puts the same amount of time into all of his classes, and he is unsure why he does so much better at some than at others. His teachers know that he is receiving some pressure at home from his mother, who is an engineer. He says he is working harder and harder as time goes on, but he is not getting the results he wants. His math and science teachers have both talked to him and are satisfied that it is not a problem with motivation. Ramon definitely is working to improve his grades, but it hasn't helped so far.

1 What, if any, learning and study difficulties does Ramon exhibit?

2 What would you do to try to help him with these difficulties?

3 Why do you think these would be useful approaches or methods?

Juliet and Ramon are different individuals, but they share some common difficulties. Although they appear to be "good" students—they work hard, are well liked, and have parental support—in some areas they are not making the grades one might expect. Juliet has problems reading. Ramon has problems with science and math. In both cases, their problems could be related to difficulties with acquiring knowledge and checking their understanding. Unfortunately, both of them may be heading toward serious academic and motivational problems in school if these learning difficulties are not addressed soon.

Juliet and Ramon are typical examples of the students teachers encounter every day in schools all across the United States. The more that teachers are learning about delinquency, school dropouts, and the learning and studying difficulties of students at risk for academic problems and failure, the more we are understanding the critical role played by student learning and study strategies in helping students reach their academic goals (Pintrich & De Groot, 1990; Pressley, Borkowski, & Schneider, 1987; Schunk, 1989; Weinstein & McCombs, in press; Zimmerman, 1990). Teachers all across the country have asked for help in both understanding and teaching students effective ways to study and learn. This book was written in response to those requests.

OVERVIEW OF THE BOOK

The last decade has witnessed an explosion in educational psychology's understanding of how students learn and study. One result of this has been the development of powerful instructional strategies that can help teachers assist students in developing the knowledge and skills needed to be effective learners who can play a more active role in their own education (Gall, Gall, Jacobsen, & Bullock, 1990; Guthrie et al., 1996; Jones & Idol, 1990; Manning, 1995; Puntambekar, 1995; Rosenshine, 1995; Shapley, 1995). This book focuses on providing an understanding of learning and study strategies and on making suggestions about ideas and tools you can use to enhance your teaching of these strategies. The target audience for this book is teachers of elementary and junior high school students. Not all of the examples and activities will be appropriate for every grade or every student, but they are designed to give you ideas and guidance for adapting them to your own situation and your students' needs.

We begin by explaining what it means to be a strategic learner and providing a brief description of a model of strategic learning and studying. This is followed by a more in-depth description of the skill domain of this model and the types of knowledge associated with this domain. The next section describes the three categories of learning and study strategies: rehearsal, elaboration, and organization. This is followed by an overview of the nature of instruction in learning and study strategies and specific methods for helping students to acquire the knowledge and skills needed to be a strategic learner. This is followed by a section designed to help you help your students develop a more systematic approach to learning and studying. Issues related to assessment and strategic planning also are discussed in this section. At the end of the book, a final review listing many of the key points is provided. To help you with terms you may not know, a glossary is provided after the final review. A bibliography of sources to help you further investigate the ideas and suggestions presented in this book is also provided.

It is our hope that this book will help you to build on your own knowledge, skills, and experience in the area of student learning and study strategies. The more active you are in your role as reader, reactor, and synthesizer, the more you will get out of the book, and the better you will be able to adapt these ideas and suggestions to your needs and the needs of your students. A number of activities have been provided for your own use and as jumping-off points for the development of curriculum materials and exercises for your students.

STATEMENT OF RATIONALE AND GOALS

Rationale

Student learning and study strategies play a crucial role in helping to determine what students learn in school and how successful they are at becoming life-long learners. Given the national concerns about retaining students in schools and enhancing student learning, it is important that every teacher knows how to help students become more effective learners. It is in response to these concerns that this book was written.

Goals

Our goals for what you will accomplish by reading and completing the exercises in this book are as follows:

1. Increased understanding of the nature of learning and study strategies and how they fit in a general model of strategic learning

2. Increased understanding of the nature and use of the three types of learning and study strategies: rehearsal, elaboration, and organizational

3. Increased understanding of the nature of instruction in learning and study strategies and your role in this process as a classroom teacher, emphasizing knowledge and ideas for how to teach students individual learning and study strategies

4. Increased knowledge and ideas for helping students to develop more systematic approaches to learning and studying that will help them to take more responsibility for their own learning, leading to their development as effective and efficient lifelong learners

goal 1

Defining Strategic Learning

There are strategic learners and struggling learners in every classroom. Although teachers may focus efforts on helping the students who are having trouble, they may be better able to help by looking to the strategic learners for a deeper understanding of what it takes to be successful. There are certain skills, attitudes, beliefs, behaviors, and ways of thinking that typify successful learners. In this chapter, we outline the characteristics of strategic learners and present a model of strategic learning that includes three key components: skill, will, and self-regulation. This goal focuses on the knowledge subset of the skill component. We outline the five types of knowledge that strategic learners must have: strategy, self-, task, content, and context knowledge.

WHAT IS A STRATEGIC LEARNER?

All teachers can think of examples of strategic learners they have seen in their own classrooms. These learners approach educational activities or tasks with a high degree of confidence that they can do the tasks, or at least with a sense that they have a good idea of how to try to complete them. Such learners are diligent and resourceful in their efforts and do not give up easily, even in the face of difficulty. They know that learning is an active process and that they must take some of the responsibility for doing it. Strategic learners actively engage the material and have some sense of when they know it and, perhaps more important, when they do not. When they encounter problems they try to find what they need to solve them, or they seek help from the teacher or classmates. They view studying and learning as a systematic process that is, to a good degree, under their control (Paris, Lipson, & Wixson, 1983; Pintrich & De Groot, 1990; Pressley & McCormick, 1995; Weinstein, Husman, & Dierking, in press; Zimmerman, 1990).

Although all teachers have experienced working with students like this, it is helpful to take a more systematic look at the characteristics of strategic learners both to gain a deeper understanding and to help derive instructional strategies to help students who may not be strategic learners. The specific definitions researchers use to explain strategic learning vary, but there are common threads and conclusions that we will focus on in our discussion. Research by Pat Alexander (e.g., Alexander & Judy, 1988), Barbara McCombs (e.g., 1994), Bill McKeachie (e.g., 1994), Scott Paris (e.g., Paris & Newman, 1990), Paul Pintrich (e.g., Pintrich & De Groot, 1990), Mike Pressley (e.g., Pressley & Associates, 1993), Dale Schunk (e.g., Schunk & Zimmerman, 1997), Merl Wittrock (Wittrock & Alesandrini, 1990), and Barry Zimmerman (e.g., Zimmerman, Bonner, & Kovach, 1996), among others, has clarified and refined strategic-learning concepts. Building on this work, C. E. Weinstein has developed a model of strategic learning that captures much of the current thinking, research results, and application data in this area (Weinstein, 1994; Weinstein et al., in press). Fundamentally, strategic learners have the *skill* to learn successfully.

1. They know a lot about how to study.

2. They use study and learning strategies.

3. They use thinking skills.

But knowing what to do is not enough. Students must have also the *will* or desire to want to use these skills and processes.

1. They must value the skills and processes.

2. They must be interested enough to be motivated to want to use them.

3. They must believe that they can use these skills and processes.

Finally, they must be *self-regulated* in order to be able to manage their own learning.

1. They can complete activities in a reasonable amount of time.

2. They plan how to meet their goals.

3. They monitor themselves to see how they are progressing.

4. They evaluate the results based on their goals and the feedback they receive from the teacher or instructional materials.

5. They take a systematic approach to learning and studying.

All of these components work interactively to impact learning outcomes and durability over time.

THE SKILL DOMAIN

In the model presented in this book, these three major sets of components are referred to as *skill, will,* and *self-regulation.* The will and self-regulation components are discussed in other books in this series (McCombs & Pope, 1994; Paris & Ayres, 1994; Zimmerman et al. 1996). Portions of the skill component are discussed also in other Psychology in the Classroom books (e.g., Sternberg & Spear-Swerling, 1996). The focus in this book is on a subset of the skill components, particularly as they affect the acquisition and use of learning and study strategies. There are a number of things students must know about and be able to use to be strategic learners who use study and learning strategies and methods effectively. The types of knowledge that students need fall into five broad categories: (a) knowledge about different learning and study strategies and how to use them (*strategy knowledge*), (b) knowledge of themselves as learners (*self-knowledge*), (c) knowledge about different types of school activities and tasks and what it means to complete them successfully (*task knowledge*), (d) current knowledge in the content area (*content knowledge*), and (e) knowledge of the context in which the learning is taking place (*context knowledge*).

Strategy Knowledge

Now let's examine the knowledge about different types of learning and study strategies that students need to have and how they must use them to meet learning goals. Knowing about and using learning and study strategies are central to the concept of strategic learning. Students must be able (and willing) to take more of the responsibility for their own knowledge acquisition and skill development. Thus an important part of teaching is helping students to negotiate the transfer of responsibility for learning from the teacher to the student. Helping students to develop and use effective and efficient learning strategies is an important step in this process. Not only does it help students to reach their current learning goals, but it is also an important building block for developing lifelong learning skills for meeting personal and occupational learning goals.

Let's begin by thinking about the different kinds of learning strategies students can use for studying and learning new information and skills. Basically, a *learning strategy* is any behavior, thought, or action a learner engages in during learning that is intended to influence the acquisition, storage in memory, integration, or availability for future use of new knowledge and skills (Weinstein et al., in press). Ultimately, the goal of using any learning strategy is to enhance knowledge acquisition, and to do so in a manner that moves that knowledge along the memory continuum so that it is integrated with related knowledge and is available for later use in other learning, problem-solving, or reasoning tasks. The specific goal for using any particular learning strategy, however, can vary.

Teaching students about learning strategies (i.e., *strategy knowledge*) helps them to become aware of how they process new information, improve the strategies they use, learn new strategies, and develop systematic approaches to studying and learning. Most students do not think much about how they learn new things. The methods they use were not systematically developed as part of their informal or formal education. Research has indicated that the methods students use at any age are developed by trial and error, comments by a teacher, parent or sibling, or conventional wisdom. These methods, or existing preferences, that students bring with them to school or other learning situations often are not very effective or efficient for many learning tasks (Weinstein, 1978). In fact, many students will continue to use strategies that are not effective for a particular learning task partly because they do not know other strategies they could use to reach their learning goals. For example, research has shown that most students will simply reread a difficult text section or chapter to help resolve their comprehension problem (Garner, 1987). Although this is sometimes a good strategy, it is often not enough to resolve the problem. However, many students will just continue rereading (or give up) because they do not know what else they can do to build knowledge from text or what the criteria would be for choosing a different strategy.

Students need to become aware of the many and different ways that they can process information. They must learn how to evaluate the effectiveness of different strategies for different learning situations, goals, and contexts. Strategic learners know how to make choices about how to learn and have a repertoire of strategies they can select from to implement these choices. Teachers need to provide more systematic instruction in learning strategies so that students can explore and discover the methods that work best for them to meet various learning demands and goals.

Take a few moments and brainstorm about different types of learning and study strategies that would be useful to students for reaching learning goals. Write down your ideas in the space below. (Use a separate piece of paper if you need more space.)

1.

2.

3.

4.

5.

6.

7.

8.

Any others?

Self-Knowledge

Strategic learners are aware of personal characteristics that can impact the difficulty or ease of learning. This knowledge of oneself as a learner is called *self-knowledge*. For example, there are several things these learners know about themselves:

1. Strategic learners know about their likes and dislikes.
   What are their favorite subjects or activities?
   What are the ones they do not like?

2. They know what kinds of tasks are easier or harder for them to accomplish.
   What has been easy for them to do in the past?
   What tasks have been difficult for them?

3. They know about their abilities.
   Where do their talents lie?
   Where do they experience difficulties?

4. They are aware of the ways they like to learn.
   What are their learning preferences (or styles)?
   What types of learning activities are fun for them?

5. They are aware of their learning strategies and study skills.
   What do they know about using learning strategies?
   Can they adapt their strategies for different tasks?
   What do they know about study habits and skills, and what are their
   current study practices?

These different kinds of knowledge and insights help strategic learners to think about and allocate resources for studying and for learning. Knowledge about oneself as a learner (*self-knowledge*) helps students to know when they need to work harder or more thoughtfully on learning tasks. If learners are working on a subject that they do not particularly enjoy and have had difficulty with before, they may need to set aside more time to work on it, change the types of strategies they have used to work on similar tasks in the past, go for help, or work with other students.

As teachers we need to help our students become more aware of themselves as learners. We need to help them learn about themselves so that they can better manage outside learning resources, such as asking us for help or working with another student, or internal resources, such as the types of learning strategies they use. We talk about specific instructional approaches more in Goal 2.

Task Knowledge

Now let's examine the knowledge students need to have about different educational activities and tasks (such as completing math problems, completing puzzles, reading, and listening in class).

Strategic learners know about typical educational activities and tasks and understand what is required to complete them successfully. It is difficult to complete a puzzle if one does not know that successfully completing a puzzle means putting all of the pieces where they belong. Similarly, older students often have difficulty with reading school materials because they do not know how to identify main ideas or what to do to help themselves remember them (Van Hout Wolters, 1994). Listening in class is difficult if one is not sure what information she or he is supposed to be focusing on when the teacher or other students talk. It is difficult to study for an essay test if one has never taken one before or does not understand how to formulate an appropriate answer. For students, working on an educational activity when they do not understand its nature or the appropriate outcome (i.e., the *task*) is like taking a trip with no idea of where they are supposed to be going or how they are supposed to get there.

An important part of teaching is helping students understand the nature of academic tasks in addition to helping them to learn how to complete the tasks successfully. This is particularly true for students who may come from an educationally impoverished background or a background with a limited range of educational experiences. Students need to know about the nature of academic tasks and the types of strategies that will help them to accomplish different tasks. The more students know about the nature and appropriate outcomes of educational tasks, and the more extensive a student's repertoire of learning and study strategies for completing those tasks, the more likely they will be successful when encountering a new learning task (Paris & Newman, 1990; Weinstein et al., in press). Conversely, if students are unclear about the nature of a particular task or activity, then it will be difficult for them to select the appropriate strategies for completing it.

Content Knowledge

Let's move on to the role of existing content knowledge in helping strategic learners to build meaning and select appropriate strategies and study skills for what they are trying to learn.

Strategic learners build bridges between what they already know and what they are trying to learn. Research has shown that these bridges make it easier to understand new information and to transfer it to more permanent memory (Mayer, 1996; Wittrock, 1990). If people have lots of connections to something in memory, then they will have many paths that they can use to find it in the future. If people have only one path to reach something, then it is far less likely they will find it. Thinking about other things people know and relating those things to what they are trying to learn help people to build these paths. A number of learning strategies build on this finding. For example, using analogies to help understand something unfamiliar and comparing and contrasting what a person knows to what he or she is trying to learn are two instances of using existing knowledge to help build meaning for something a person is trying to learn.

It is important for teachers to help students learn how to use their existing (*content*) knowledge to build bridges to things they are trying to learn. Research has shown that many students do not know how to build meaning (Pressley & McCormick, 1995). As teachers, we can provide information, but only students can transform it and generate their own knowledge. The more we can teach them how to build meaning for whatever they are trying to learn, the more capable they will be of independent, self-directed learning. Helping students to use knowledge they already have to build meaning is a big step in this direction. Many learning strategies, such as the use of analogies, comparison and contrast, application, and the building of direct relationships, require the use of prior knowledge to help make the new information more meaningful. If students do not know how to use prior knowledge to build bridges to new information, they will not be able to effectively use these strategies. Teachers must help students to become more aware of their prior relevant knowledge and the ways in which they can use it to build bridges to what they are trying to learn.

Context Knowledge

Now let's examine how knowing about the context, the social setting, and the environment in which learning is taking place can help students be more strategic learners. *Context variables* include but are not limited to

☐ teacher expectations

☐ time constraints for assignments

☐ school behavior expectations and norms

☐ peer interactions and support

Strategic learners are aware of the context in which they are learning and how that context frames, constrains, and supports studying and learning (i.e., *context knowledge*). For example, they understand school and classroom norms for both behavior and achievement. They are aware of task and project deadlines and know how to use this information to help them plan their efforts toward task achievement. They know about resources available to them in the classroom and school environment, such as the library and teacher aides or tutors, and how to use them as resources to help reach learning goals. They also create a social network of support in the classroom (Paris & Newman, 1990).

Context variables help students to know what is expected of them by teachers and peers, available resources for accomplishing learning tasks, and the level of support or encouragement they can expect. These variables have strong relationships to the selection and use of learning strategies, particularly for working on difficult or challenging tasks. If students feel supported and encouraged they are more likely to work on difficult tasks and to try a variety of learning strategies (Pintrich & Schunk, 1996). If they understand the constraints of time and resources for an assignment or school task, they can use this information to select a reasonable strategy, one that will not require more resources than are available. If they are clear on what is required of them and expectations about successful performance, then it is easier for them to select strategies to reach these goals. For example, it has been found that students in classes where the teacher effectively communicates expectations for higher or deeper levels of understanding tend to use more, and more complex, learning strategies (Ames & Archer, 1988).

As teachers, we need to help our students become more aware of context variables and how to use this information to set and reach their learning goals. Understanding the school and classroom environment gives students an edge on making the environment work for them. The types of strategies they choose and use will be affected by this knowledge.

We have presented five different types of knowledge students need to have to be strategic learners: strategy knowledge, self-knowledge, task knowledge, content knowledge, and context knowledge. One way to deepen your own understanding of the importance of these five types of knowledge is to reflect on how you use them to meet your own learning goals, in addition to how they might help your students to become more effective and efficient learners.

I Take a few moments and think about how you learn new things. Think about ways that the five types of knowledge impact your learning.

1. How does strategy knowledge help you to learn?

2. How does self-knowledge help you to learn?

3. How does task knowledge help you to learn?

4. How does content knowledge help you to learn?

5. How does context knowledge help you to learn?

II Now think of a lesson you will be teaching your students.

1. How might their strategy knowledge affect the ways they will try to learn the material?

2. How might their self-knowledge affect the ways they will try to learn the material?

3. How might their task knowledge affect the ways they will try to learn the material?

4. How might their content knowledge affect the ways they will try to learn the material?

5. How might their context knowledge affect the ways they will try to learn the material?

Reflect back on the learning strategies you used to learn the information presented in this first part of this book. Write down a few examples in the space below and then describe why you think this was (or wasn't) a useful strategy for you.

1 Strategy

Why it was (or wasn't) useful for you:

2 Strategy

Why it was (or wasn't) useful for you:

3 Strategy

Why it was (or wasn't) useful for you:

4 Strategy

Why it was (or wasn't) useful for you:

5 Strategy

Why it was (or wasn't) useful for you:

6 Any others?

Now that we have discussed the general nature of learning strategies and how they fit within the skill component in a model of strategic learning, let's turn our attention to a more in-depth look at the categories and characteristics of learning and study strategies in Goal 2.

SUGGESTED READINGS

McKeachie, W. J. (1994). *Teaching tips* (9th ed.). Lexington, MA: Heath.

Weinstein, C. E., & Mayer, R. E. (1986). The teaching of learning strategies. In M. C. Wittrock (Ed.), *Handbook of research on teaching* (3rd ed., pp. 315–327). New York: Macmillan

Zimmerman, B. J., & Schunk, D. H. (Eds.). (1989). *Self-regulated learning and academic achievement: Theory, research, and practice.* New York: Springer-Verlag.

goal 2

Understanding the Categories and

Characteristics of Learning Strategies

To foster a better understanding of strategic learning, we present a system to classify the strategies and a vocabulary to describe them. This goal begins by outlining the three common categories used to describe learning strategies: *rehearsal, elaboration,* and *organizational strategies.* Weinstein and Mayer (1986) developed these categories to apply to both basic learning tasks—knowledge acquisition and comprehension—and complex learning tasks—application, analysis, and synthesis. Next, we outline the three kinds of knowledge that learners need to effectively acquire, select, and use learning strategies: *declarative*, *procedural*, and *conditional knowledge*. Finally, we introduce pre-, during-, and posttask strategies.

REHEARSAL STRATEGIES FOR BASIC LEARNING TASKS

Rehearsal strategies use active repetition to hold onto something in memory. *Rehearsing* means the learner is actively reciting or naming what he or she is trying to remember. In its simplest form, rehearsal is used to maintain something in temporary memory until it is used. For example, if you have ever called information for a phone number and then quickly repeated it to yourself until you dialed the number, you were using a simple rehearsal strategy. These strategies can be used also to facilitate transfer to long-term memory, such as when people repeat someone's name over and over again so that they begin to attach it to that person.

Rehearsal strategies for basic learning tasks focus on repetition to increase familiarity and memory. Rehearsal strategies usually involve repeating key terms or items aloud, rereading, repetitive writing, or using mnemonic devices such as tunes, rhymes, and pictures. They include actions such as repeating the letters of the alphabet using the common tune that children sing, saying rhymes to remember the steps for clearning up the classroom and putting all of the toys away at the end of the school day, and reciting the names of the planets in the order of their distance from earth. Each of these methods is designed to help people learn and remember new things or procedures. Over time, people may not need to use these strategies as the information they are repeating becomes a part of their knowledge base (although we still know many adults who must use the ABC song to help them remember the order of individual letters in the alphabet!).

REHEARSAL STRATEGIES FOR COMPLEX LEARNING TASKS

When dealing with more complex learning tasks, such as studying a chapter of text or taking notes in a class, rehearsal strategies can take some additional forms and be used for additional purposes. Rehearsal strategies for complex learning tasks can help students focus their attention on main ideas and important portions of a reading and help them to learn and remember this information. For example, when you highlight key information in a journal or magazine, take selective notes in a seminar, or copy useful information from a teacher's guide, you are using rehearsal strategies. You are using some form of repetition for a limited number of items to help create further occasions for learning to take place.

Rehearsal strategies for complex learning tasks focus on selection of important information and repetition to increase familiarity, understanding, and memory. Rehearsal strategies for complex learning tasks involve more active thinking on the part of the student. For example, to rehearse important information from a textbook, the student must be able to select main ideas and separate didactic information from the key things they must understand and hold on to in memory. If a student is using a note-taking strategy to record information from the textbook or a class, then the student must select both which information to copy and the form the notes will take (e.g., straight copying, branching diagram, or ordered list).

Common examples of the use of rehearsal strategies for complex tasks include repeating information aloud (*shadowing*), taking selective notes, underlining important information, highlighting parts of a text, and copying material. Although rehearsal strategies do help students to select and acquire information, they do not generally help students to integrate that information with other things that they know, or to build bridges among parts of what they are learning. A knowledge base full of independent and discrete information is not very useful as a tool for further learning or as a resource for higher order thinking and application. The next category of learning strategies, elaboration strategies, addresses these problems.

Think about your own content area(s). How can rehearsal strategies best be used by your students to meet their learning goals for the basic learning tasks you present?

☐ Think of two basic learning tasks that you teach. Now think about which rehearsal strategies might best help your students to accomplish these tasks.

Describe a basic learning task from one of your lessons.

What rehearsal strategies might help your students to complete this task successfully?
1.
2.
3.
Any others?

Describe a second basic learning task from one of your lessons.

What rehearsal strategies might help your students to complete this task successfully?
1.
2.
3.
Any others?

II Now think of two complex learning tasks you teach. Think about which rehearsal strategies might best help your students to accomplish these tasks.

Describe a complex learning task from one of your lessons.

What rehearsal strategies might help your students to complete this task successfully?
1.
2.
3.
Any others?

Describe a second complex learning task from one of your lessons.

What rehearsal strategies might help your students to complete this task successfully?
1.
2.
3.
Any others?

ELABORATION STRATEGIES FOR BASIC LEARNING TASKS

Elaboration strategies help students to build bridges between what they already know and what they are trying to learn and remember. By elaborating on or adding to the material, students build up meaning and help to move the new information along the memory continuum. Using these strategies also helps students to organize and integrate their new and old knowledge in meaningful ways. This not only helps to make the new information more understandable and memorable but also helps to generate a usable data base for higher order thinking and application. Using elaboration strategies helps students to learn and store information in a usable form. Teachers know that as students gain more knowledge in an area, it is important for them to be able to integrate their knowledge as a step toward developing greater expertise in using it. Elaboration learning strategies help them to reach this goal.

In their simplest form, elaboration strategies can be used to learn lists of conceptually related items or meaningful relationships among a group of items. For example, if you were trying to remember that a tomato is a fruit, you might create a mental image of a tomato sitting in a bowl of fruit, imagine that you are eating a bowl of fruit with tomatoes in it, or make up a sentence explaining why a tomato is a fruit. Each of these strategies would help to begin building meaning for what you are trying to learn and relate it to associated knowledge.

Elaboration strategies for basic learning tasks focus on building bridges either among parts of what students are trying to learn or between what they are trying to learn and their prior content knowledge. Although these strategies have their greatest impact with complex learning materials, they are also useful for simple tasks such as learning foreign vocabulary, serial lists, and clusters of items. Relating a foreign vocabulary word to English forms of the word, exploring the relationships among scientific terms, and generating an image of a scene described in a story are all forms of elaboration strategies for basic learning tasks. The bridges students build using these strategies help them to cross back and forth between their existing knowledge and the new information.

ELABORATION STRATEGIES FOR COMPLEX LEARNING TASKS

The real power of elaboration strategies is most evident when they are used to help with mastering complex learning tasks. These strategies can range from students simply restating the information using their own words to teaching it to someone else or using it to solve a problem. Each of these methods is designed to deepen a student's understanding of the new information and store it in memory with related knowledge. When you think about how a new teaching idea relates to other ways you teach similar material, paraphrase an article, or translate research results into concrete suggestions for your work, you are using elaboration strategies. You are adding to what you are trying to learn and remember in order to help give it more meaning for you and make it easier to remember and use.

Elaboration strategies for complex learning tasks focus on selection of important information for further study and building meaning for this information by relating it to what is already known or using reasoning skills to analyze it and build internal connections and meaning. Students cannot be mentally passive and use elaboration learning strategies. They require a lot of cognitive effort to be effective. In fact, research has shown that part of the benefit students derive from using elaboration learning strategies comes from both the processing itself and the products that result (Gagné, 1985). When students use elaboration learning strategies, they are actively interacting with the material. This helps to increase attention, concentration, and interest.

Common examples of the use of elaboration strategies for complex tasks include summarizing in one's own words, paraphrasing, doing *generative* note taking (paraphrasing and expanding on the material in the notes versus taking verbatim notes, which is a rehearsal strategy), asking and answering questions about the material, teaching it to someone else, comparing and contrasting, and analyzing the relationships among components. We discuss more examples in Goals 3 and 4.

Think about your own content area(s). How can elaboration strategies best be used by your students to meet their learning goals for basic learning tasks you present?

I. Think of two basic learning tasks you teach. Now think about which elaboration strategies might best help your students to accomplish these tasks.

Describe a basic learning task from one of your lessons.

What elaboration strategies might help your students to complete this task successfully?
1.
2.
3.
Any others?

Describe a second basic learning task from one of your lessons.

Which elaboration strategies might help your students to complete this task successfully?
1.
2.
3.
Any others?

II Think of two complex learning tasks you teach. Now think about which elaboration strategies might best help your students to accomplish these tasks.

Describe a complex learning task from one of your lessons.

Which elaboration strategies might help your students to complete this task success-fully?
1.
2.
3.
Any others?

Describe a second complex learning task from one of your lessons.

Which elaboration strategies might help your students to complete this task success-fully?
1.
2.
3.
Any others?

ORGANIZATIONAL STRATEGIES FOR BASIC LEARNING TASKS

Organizational strategies are a specialized form of elaboration strategies. However, they are so commonly used and are so powerful that most classifications of learning strategies separate them out into their own category (e.g., Pressley & McCormick, 1995; Schunk, 1996). These strategies involve imposing an organizational framework onto the information students are trying to learn. This framework can be specific to the new information (an *internal organization*) or can relate it to existing knowledge (an *elaborated framework*). In their simplest form, organizational strategies often focus on clustering new information to make it more manageable or easier to remember.

Clustering can help take some of the load off what is often referred to as *working memory*. Science doesn't yet understand the limits to human memory. However, it is known that there are clear limits to the amount of information people can focus on at any particular moment in time. The working memory is the part of the human mind that can be conceptualized metaphorically as a work area, like a conference table or desk (Baddeley, 1992). Researchers have found that people can keep about 9 things in working memory simultaneously (Miller, 1956). The things, or *chunks,* of information that people can keep in working memory can vary tremendously in size. Thus one of the ways people can expand their working space is by chunking things into bigger pieces. This is one of the goals of using organizational strategies. They help people to cluster information into bigger chunks. For example, cover the rest of this page while you try to memorize the following string of letters:

TwauSAibMUniCeF

Think about how easy or difficult you found this task and why. Most people would have difficulty remembering a string of 15 meaningless letters without doing something to give the letters some organization or meaning. One of the ways you may have done this with the list we just presented was by clustering the items. For example, here is one possible clustering:

TWA   USA   IBM   UNICEF

Clustering the letters in this way reduces the memory load from 15 isolated things (letters) to 4 isolated things (common acronyms). This example demonstrates how organizational learning strategies can reduce the load on working memory. This is a major function of organizational strategies for basic learning tasks.

Organizational strategies for basic learning tasks focus on reducing the load on working memory and helping to build meaning for the new information students are trying to learn (Basden, Basden, Devecchio, & Anders, 1991). When students use organizational strategies, they often chunk things together into larger clusters or impose a conceptual framework on a set of items. They include strategies such as classifying items into animal, vegetable, or mineral categories; identifying the hierarchical relationships in mathematics; diagramming a section of a textbook; and clustering major battles of World War II into time segments (Ericsson & Polson, 1988).

ORGANIZATIONAL STRATEGIES FOR COMPLEX LEARNING TASKS

When dealing with more complex learning tasks, organizational strategies not only help to reduce the memory load but also play a big role in helping to make the information more meaningful and easier to incorporate into memory, so that it can be retrieved and used in the future (Schunk, 1996). For example, using the typical components of a story to help organize the actions and flow of events makes it not only easier to maintain in working memory but also helps to build meaning for the tale.

Organizational strategies for complex learning tasks help to expand working memory capacity while they help students to build meaning for the new information and move it along the memory continuum so the information is available for future use. Like elaboration learning strategies, these strategies require that students actively think about the material and focus their attention on the key things they must understand and hold on to in memory.

Common examples of the use of organizational strategies for complex tasks include diagramming text, sorting new paintings into existing categories, creating a tree diagram to summarize the main ideas and their interrelations from a class unit, and creating a conditional flowchart to explain a complex production process. All of these methods help to generate meaning and reduce the working memory load, so that students can concentrate their efforts on understanding and using the new material (Klatzky, 1980).

Think about your own content area(s). How can organizational strategies best be used by your students to meet their learning goals for basic learning tasks you present?

I Think of two basic learning tasks you teach. Now think about which organizational strategies might best help your students to accomplish these tasks.

Describe a basic learning task from one of your lessons.

Which organizational strategies might help your students to complete the task successfully?
1.
2.
3.

Any others?

Describe a second basic learning task from one of your lessons.

Which organizational strategies might help your students to complete this task successfully?
1.
2.
3.

Any others?

II Now think of two complex learning tasks you teach. Think about which organizational strategies might best help your students to accomplish these tasks.

Describe a complex learning task from one of your lessons.

Which organizational strategies might help your students to complete this task successfully?
1.
2.
3.

Any others?

Describe a second complex learning task from one of your lessons.

Which organizational strategies might help your students to complete this task successfully?
1.
2.
3.

Any others?

Note that people often do not just use one or another of these strategies. It is much more common to use combinations or mixtures. Strategic learners are able to self-regulate by selecting and integrating strategies appropriate to the specific learning goals. For example, consider the following case: Charlie is studying the scientific method in his seventh-grade science class. When first introduced to this topic, he uses a rehearsal strategy—repeating aloud—to memorize the steps in the process (e.g., "generate a hypothesis, test, retest, proof"). While still learning the steps by name, he uses the elaboration strategy of compare and contrast to distinguish the various steps from each other. Finally, he uses an organizational strategy to help build deeper meaning by chunking the steps of the scientific process into bigger theoretical pieces. Although he uses these strategies somewhat sequentially—it wouldn't make sense for Charlie to "chunk" the steps before being able to distinguish among them—he also uses these strategies simultaneously.

A Preliminary List of Rehearsal, Elaboration, and Organizational Strategies

For Memorization

Rehearsal strategies	Using mnemonic devices
	Reading material over again
	Writing material over again
	Repeating key terms aloud
	Using notecards
	Taking notes verbatim
	Saying material over and over

For Meaningful Learning

Elaboration strategies	Assimilating new material into existing knowledge organizations
	Making new conceptual frameworks for new material (accommodation)
	Paraphrasing
	Summarizing
	Creating analogies
	Asking or answering questions about the material
	Teaching the material to someone else
	Applying knowledge in new situations

A Preliminary List of Rehearsal, Elaboration, and Organizational Strategies

For Meaningful Learning (*Continued*)

Organizational strategies	Outlining
	Diagramming
	Classifying
	Categorizing
	Noting similarities and differences
	Identifying hierarchical
	relationships
	Separating main ideas from details

DECLARATIVE, PROCEDURAL, AND CONDITIONAL KNOWLEDGE ABOUT STRATEGIES

Researchers talk about three general types of knowledge that strategic learners need to effectively acquire, select, and use learning strategies to meet their learning goals: *declarative, procedural,* and *conditional* knowledge (Anderson, 1990; Paris et al., 1983; Pressley and Afflerbach, 1995; Weinstein & McCombs, in press).

Declarative Knowledge About Learning Strategies

Declarative knowledge is what students need to know about different strategies and their characteristics. Acquiring declarative knowledge about learning strategies helps students to become aware of different types of strategies and to learn about their individual characteristics and uses. For example, when discussing a rehearsal strategy for basic tasks, a teacher could tell students, "It helps to repeat things we are trying to remember. When you repeat things, it means you say them over and over to yourself. Have you ever repeated someone's name so you could remember it? Have you ever repeated the instructions for a game, so you would remember how to play it? By repeating things like this, we help ourselves to remember them. So, what is one way we can help ourselves to remember things? (Wait for a response.) That's right, by saying them over and over to ourselves."

Let's look at an example of declarative knowledge for an elaboration strategy for complex tasks. The teacher is discussing how to use analogies (the declarative knowledge is in italics).

> Sometimes it is difficult for us to understand something we are trying to learn. There are many things we can use to help ourselves when this happens. *One way is to find something else*

that is similar, although not the same, and use it to build our understanding. If you were just learning about our memory and how it works, it might be difficult to get the basic concept. However, it would be easier if you could think about something else you know more about that is similar to human memory. You could use those similarities to help you understand human memory better. For example, if you have ever been in an office, you have seen a filing cabinet. There are a lot of similarities between how a filing cabinet is organized and how our memories are organized. Filing cabinets hold a lot of information, and so can our memory. Filing cabinets have a number of different drawers and places where we can store information, and so does our memory. Filing cabinets are easier to use when that information is organized in some way (like putting your notes from science class in the same drawer), and it is easier for us to get information from memory if we can "store" similar things together.

Thinking about these similarities helps to make the idea of human memory more meaningful and easier to understand and remember. *When we look for similarities between things that are alike but not exactly the same, we say we are creating analogies. We say something is similar (or analogous) to something else. We usually do this when we are trying to help ourselves to understand and remember something we want to learn. We use something we already know to help us better understand something we are trying to learn.* You may have noticed that I use a lot of analogies when I am teaching you new things. Can anyone remember an analogy we used in class recently? (Wait for a response.) Yes, that is a good one! You can use analogies to help yourself learn new things you are studying in school or on your own. They are wonderful learning strategies that can help you to make sense of new concepts or ideas.

Although knowing about learning strategies and their characteristics is an important part of the knowledge students need, it is not sufficient. Students must also learn how to use these strategies to help them with different learning situations. Educators learned a lot about teaching in college classes, but it was not until we stepped into the classroom and began to learn how to apply that knowledge that we really began to develop our expertise. It is important that teachers tell our students about learning strategies, but it is also critical that we help them to develop expertise in using them.

Procedural Knowledge About Learning Strategies

Once students know about strategies and their characteristics, it is important to move quickly on to teaching them how to use these strategies. In fact, research has shown that it is better to present a minimal amount of declarative knowledge and then move on quickly to discussing procedural knowledge, giving students a chance to practice using the strategies (Gagné, 1985). We discuss this further in the section on teaching methods.

Conditional Knowledge About Learning Strategies

As students gain expertise in using learning strategies, it is important that they learn about the conditions under which it is or is not useful to use a particular strategy (Zimmerman, 1989, 1990). For example, you would generally not use *text mapping* (diagramming important information and relationships) while reading a newspaper article (unless it was for an assignment or project report), but you might use it for a difficult or important section of text. Learning about the strengths and limitations of different strategies and refining their understanding of how each strategy works and why it can be helpful are important tasks for students. Teachers can play an important role in this process by both teaching about these issues and giving students feedback not only on their performance but also on how they went about learning what they needed to know to do it.

PRE-, DURING-, AND POSTTASK STRATEGIES

Whereas conditional knowledge helps students recognize when a certain stratgy is appropriate for a particular task, students should also know that strategies can be used before, during, and after learning tasks. We refer to these as *pre-, during,* and *poststrategies.*

Prestrategies help to set the stage. Prestrategies include having the appropriate materials and being in the appropriate frame of mind. *During strategies* are strategies that are aimed at building new meaning for new information, to help people learn it. Most of the strategies discussed previously in this chapter would be appropriate to use during this knowledge-acquisition phase. *Poststrategies* focus on checking understanding or comprehension monitoring.

Using pre-, during, and poststrategies allows students to select strategies for different purposes. If they paraphrase a section of text while reading it, they are building meaning and learning the content. If they paraphrase a passage while reviewing the chapter, they are checking on their comprehension and making sure that it is accurate and adequate. (We discuss these strategies more in Goals 3 and 4.) The following list provides some pre-, during, and poststrategies for the task of reading.

Pre-, During-, and Postreading Strategies

Prereading strategies	Have the appropriate materials.
	Determine what the task is. Why did the teacher assign it?
	Determine the author's purpose in writing the story.
	Skim to get a general idea of the content.
	Develop questions to be answered while reading.
During-reading strategies	Find an appropriate reading speed.
	Look for main ideas and details.
	Notice how this fits with what you already know.
	Take notes on the reading in outline form.
	Summarize the story.
	Use other knowledge-acquisition strategies.
Postreading strategies	Write and answer some "typical" test questions.
	Try teaching the material to a classmate.
	Try to draw a picture representing the material.
	Summarize the reading in your own words.

Now that we have presented a set of knowledge and terms to understand and explain learning and study strategies, it is time to focus on how best to teach the prerequisite knowledge and skills students need, to become strategic lifelong learners. Let's turn to Goal 3.

SUGGESTED READINGS

Gall, M. D., Gall, J. P., Jacobsen, D. R., & Bullock, T. L. (1990). *Tools for learning*. Alexandria, VA: Association for Supervision and Curriculum Development.

Weinstein, C. E. (1994). Strategic learning/strategic teaching: Flip sides of a coin. In P. R. Pintrich, D. R. Brown, & C. E. Weinstein (Eds.), *Student motivation, cognition, and learning: Essays in honor of Wilbert J. McKeachie (pp. 257–273)*. Hillsdale, NJ: Erlbaum.

Understanding How to Teach Learning and Study Strategies

Goal 1 of this book focused on helping you to increase your knowledge base about the nature of learning and study strategies and how these strategies fit into a general model of strategic learning. Goal 2 was directed toward helping you increase your understanding of the nature and types of categories of learning and study strategies. The more you know about different types of learning strategies and methods you can use to help students become more strategic learners, the more effective you will be in the classroom. Goal 3 focuses on extending your knowledge base about how to help students learn about and use effective learning and study strategies and how this impacts your role as a teacher. We give you specific ideas of how to use this information in your classroom. We begin by identifying the three categories of teaching methods–*direct instruction, modeling,* and *guided practice with feedback.* Then we show you how to help students approach learning systematically. Finally, we provide practical suggestions about how to facilitate student awareness of the five types of knowledge.

THREE CATEGORIES OF TEACHING METHODS

There are three general categories of teaching methods for helping students to acquire and develop cognitive skills, such as using learning strategies:

1. Direct instruction

2. Modeling

3. Guided practice with feedback

Usually, teachers will use some combination of the three. *Direct instruction* (which is often used to teach the declarative knowledge discussed in the previous goal) involves telling students about the strategies and how to use them. *Modeling* (which is often used to teach procedural knowledge) requires the teacher to demonstrate how to use the strategy. *Guided practice with feedback* is usually used after direct instruction and modeling so that students can try out the strategies and get feedback about their choices and implementation (which is often used to teach conditional knowledge). This is usually done over a prolonged period so that students get a chance to continue refining their procedural and conditional strategy knowledge.

HELPING STUDENTS APPROACH LEARNING SYSTEMATICALLY

Knowing about a variety of learning strategies, learning how to use a variety of learning strategies, and knowing when and why to use a particular learning strategy are all important aspects of becoming a strategic learner. However, students must also learn how to take a systematic approach to learning and studying that helps them to embed their strategy choices in a particular context. For example, the type of note-taking strategy a seventh-grade science student would choose to use when reading the text in preparation for an upcoming test would depend on a number of factors. Students may ask themselves, what other assignments or projects are due during the same period? How much do I like science? How well have I done on other tests in this class? What type of test will it be? What grade do I want to earn on this test? How many chapters do I need to read? Adding this level of complexity requires students to take a planful and systematic approach to learning and studying.

Using a systematic approach to learning and studying helps students to become more sophisticated in their selection and use of learning strategies. It involves combining information from each of the knowledge categories (self as a learner, the nature of academic tasks, current content knowledge, current repertoire of learning strategies, and the academic context), as well as the other components of strategic learning (will and self-regulation), to approach learning tasks in a planful and systematic manner to achieve learning goals. Systematic approaches to learning are *heuristic* in nature. This means that they are not simple step-by-step procedures that can be mindlessly followed. Teachers cannot tell students how to learn everything they will need to know in each grade of school or in later life, but we can help them to develop guidelines, frameworks, and ways of thinking about learning and studying tasks that will help them to increase their chances of reaching their learning goals.

Using a systematic approach to learning and studying improves with practice over time. However, there is much that each teacher can do to help students along this pathway. Teaching students about the five types of knowledge they will need to be strategic learners is the first step. Helping them to develop increasing levels of expertise with a variety of learning strategies is also a necessary step. However, these steps by themselves are not sufficient. Students must be taught how to start combining these different types of knowledge in the face of different learning tasks and contextual constraints (such as the time available, available resources, and importance of the task). They also must become aware of the interactions among these variables and the other two components of strategic learning: skill and will.

Strategic learners need to be aware of their thought processes so that they can better organize and more efficiently and effectively use and integrate their learning and study strategies. For example, students first need to be aware of what strategies they are using to learn new material and how well those strategies are working. With that knowledge in hand, they can analyze the process and improve on those strategies at that point in time or in the future. The next scenario illustrates this point.

> **STUDENT EXAMPLE: GEORGE** George opened his second-grade reader to the story the teacher had assigned. It was about a circus bear that escaped and went to the mall. He quickly turned the pages, looking at all of the pictures. It looked like a fun story. On the last page, he noticed some questions. "Uh, oh," he thought. He read them and realized that he couldn't answer them yet, so he copied the questions on a sheet of paper and left space to fill in the right answers as he went. He started back at the beginning and looked at his sheet of paper. It read, "Who is the author of this story?" He smiled to himself and copied down the author's name. Then he noticed that no one else was using this strategy. He held up his hand until Ms. Gonzales came over. He asked her if he was doing it right, and she assured him that it was a good strategy to use. In fact, she was so impressed, she told the whole class what strategies he was using to read—*previewing the text* (looking at the pictures), *identifying the task* (finding the study questions), and *organizing the material* (copying the study questions). She then asked him how he was going to check to make sure that he got all of the right answers. He thought for a second, then replied that he could ask Stacie, who was sitting across from him. Ms. Gonzales smiled and agreed. She then asked the other students to come up with pre-, during, and poststrategies to use for reading the story. George continued reading and felt good about himself as a learner.

Through their increasing awareness and skill development, students are able to identify heuristics, or general guidelines, that can apply in many different types of learning situations. One heuristic that is simple to learn at any level and would be useful to teach explicitly in class is that learning strategies can be divided into pre-, during, and poststrategies. Prestrategies deal with preparation: What does the task require? Do I have all of the necessary materials? How can I get in the proper frame of mind for this content area?

> **STUDENT EXAMPLE: RUBY** Ruby found her seat in the class just as the bell rang. Eighth-grade science was interesting, she had decided. She had read all of the information the night before, and looking back at yesterday's notes, she saw that they were going to do an experiment today on connecting currents. She dated her notes, wrote down the topic as "Currents/Electricity," and opened her text to the right chapter. As soon as the teacher began, Ruby was ready to go.

Ruby has used some effective prestrategies. She came to class intellectually prepared by reading the appropriate material before the class and glancing over the previous day's lecture notes. She had the appropriate materials—pen, paper, and text. She also organized those materials well. She dated and labeled her notes and opened her text. Ruby was ready to move on to during strategies.

During strategies deal directly with building meaning for knowledge acquisition, or how one actually learns the content. This happens while students read, listen in class, or work problems. Any time a new concept, fact, or idea is being acquired or reinforced (when new boxes are being made or when material is being put into boxes of prior knowledge), learners use during strategies. Unfortunately, many times those strategies aren't particularly mindful. Strategic learners do a better job than nonstrategic learners of matching their strategy choices to the task requirements.

Ruby started to take notes as her teacher began talking. She quickly fell behind. She realized that she could not keep up and write down every word he said, so she tried paraphrasing. This worked better, but as he started the experiment, she saw that her notes became more and more confusing because the teacher was doing more and more and talking less and less. She knew that he wanted them to be able to make a complete circuit themselves, so instead of writing down words, Ruby began to make diagrams of what the teacher was doing. This worked much better, and Ruby felt that she could make a complete circuit by looking at her notes. When the bell rang at the end of class, Ruby felt that she had learned a lot.

Ruby, in this scenario, was aware of which strategies she was using and how effective they were. When they stopped working, for example, when she fell behind trying to take notes verbatim, she adjusted her strategy. Although that worked better, she realized that it did not fit with the task requirements— being able to make a complete circuit herself. Her teacher was asking for the students to learn the concept at an application level, and her notes were aimed more at simple comprehension. So Ruby adjusted once again to make a better match between how she was learning the information and what would be required of her later.

The last group of strategies in this approach is the poststrategies. These come after knowledge has been put into boxes. Here, the strategic learner goes back and looks to see if the information that was placed in the box was the right information and if it really belonged in the box in which it was initially placed.

After school, Ruby checked with Mark, a friend who was in science class with her, and they went over their notes. Ruby and Mark both noticed a few sections where their notes were incomplete. By putting their notes together, they were able to look for holes and discrepancies and correct them. Later that night, Ruby compared her notes with the textbook and was pleased to see that her diagrams looked much like what was written in the textbook. She saw one difference: In her notes, one of her connectors was labeled *positive* while the book labeled it as *negative*. She and Mark hadn't noticed this earlier, so she put a big question mark by it to remind herself to ask her teacher the next day. The next day, before class began, she received clarification from her teacher about her question from the night before. Ruby asked if she could use the equipment that was still out on the tables. Her teacher said she could. Using her notes, Ruby connected the wires to the battery, and sure enough, the lightbulb glowed steadily. She shut her notebook, confident that she would do well in the practical quiz later that day.

It is important to check one's comprehension after an attempt at acquiring new knowledge. Strategic learners take responsibility for this themselves. In the previous scenario, Ruby double-checked her notes, both with another student and against the book. She then got further clarification from the teacher and applied her new knowledge. An important part of teaching is checking students' comprehension. Teachers give quizzes, ask questions, require papers, and assign homework to help check students' understanding of new concepts and facts. However, an important component of strategic learning is that learners start to take responsibility for checking their understanding. Teachers have to help them learn how to do this. Using poststrategies puts learners ahead of the game. They have had an opportunity to check for any misunderstandings and correct them before the teacher administers a comprehension check. Because of this, strategic learners will often have higher grades and understand the concepts much better than their less strategic counterparts.

Now let's look at some of the ways teachers can help students to develop and integrate the five types of knowledge: knowledge of self, knowledge of tasks, knowledge of content, knowledge of strategies, and knowledge of context.

FACILITATING STUDENT AWARENESS OF THE FIVE TYPES OF KNOWLEDGE

Self-Knowledge

In order to become more strategic learners, students should have a realistic picture of who they are as learners. Teachers can help students to increase or deepen this type of knowledge in several ways. One way is through the Personal Characteristics Survey that follows this section.

It would be relatively easy to modify this activity for different instructional goals or students. For instance, this could be done as a group activity, either with the whole class or with small cooperative groups. For example, the teacher could read this survey aloud and solicit class responses. This might particularly be useful for younger children, who might not yet have the necessary reading skills. This activity could also incorporate writing and art activities. For example, you might say, "Tell me more in the story about yourself. Write a story about a day in school that you learned a lot. Describe what that day was like. Use lots of detail. Make a cover sheet for your story that has a picture of you at school doing what you like to do the very most." As a teacher, you could begin this activity by modeling what you are like as a learner. Make sure to emphasize to your students that all learners have strengths and weaknesses and that by knowing more about themselves as learners, people can improve their learning abilities.

Personal Characteristics Survey

Name: _____ page 1

Instructions: Fill in the following sentences

My favorite class is

_____

_____

My least favorite class is

_____

_____

My favorite activity at school is

_____

_____

My least favorite activity at school is

_____

_____

I think _____

is easy.

I think _____

is hard.

- -

page 2

I like to learn best by (circle one or more):

      1. listening to the teacher

      2. watching someone do something new

      3. making something with my hands

When I read, I _____

_____

to help me understand.

When I work math problems, I

_____

to help me understand.

I _____

_____

to help me remember important things.

I also do _____

to help me remember important things.

Now that you know more about yourself as a learner, tell a short story that would explain to your parents or your teacher who you are as a learner. (You may use the back of this sheet if you need more space.)

As a learner I . . .

Another aspect of self-knowledge is how effective one is as a student. Generally, teachers already have a good idea of which students are both effective and efficient in their classrooms and which students are not. For those few cases where the teacher is not sure, a quick conference with the student or parents should clarify the issue. It is important to realize when questioning a student, however, that it is common for most students to inflate the amount of time they think that they study. Conversely, those few students who are effective yet inefficient may underestimate their study time. They tend to feel that whatever they are doing is never enough. A tool to help obtain greater accuracy in student reports is a time log. The students record what they are doing at regular intervals (it can be broken down as small as 15-minute intervals or as large as 1-hour intervals). This helps them to determine exactly what they are doing with their time. This can be done using as few as 2 days for younger students (with frequent reminders to fill it out) to as much as a week with older students (who might also need several reminders). This is a valuable learning tool that enables students to see where their time is spent. It is also a helpful time-management tool that enables students to take responsibility for planning and will serve them well into adulthood.

The following form is very useful for this purpose. Students simply fill in key words or phrases, such as *watching TV, doing homework, eating,* or *being with friends.* The increased awareness of how they are spending their time is often shocking for students. It can be a powerful tool for changing beliefs and behavior.

A Week in the Life of _____

Instructions: Fill in the following schedule as thoroughly as you can

	Monday	Tuesday	Wednesday	Thursday	Friday	Saturday	Sunday
7–8							
8–9							
9–10							
10–11							
11–12							
12–1							
1–2							
2–3							
3–4							
4–5							
5–6							
6–7							

(worksheet continues)

	Monday	Tuesday	Wednesday	Thursday	Friday	Saturday	Sunday
7–8							
8–9							
9–10							
10–11							
11–12							

Task Knowledge

This may be a good time to dust off *Bloom's taxonomy* (Bloom, 1956), which is a hierarchy describing the quality of thinking processes from simple to complex (see Table 1). It is sometimes helpful to introduce this hierarchy to students, to carefully explain to them what you expect them to learn. For younger students, the teacher can share the concepts in a way that the students can understand. Teachers can share the hierarchy itself with older students. When students know specifically what the teacher expects them to know, and to what level they are to know it, they are more likely to choose appropriate strategies for learning the information.

Table 1   Bloom's Taxonomy

Level of Complexity	Hierarchical Level	Processes	Products
Very basic	1. Knowledge	remember, name, list, memorize, repeat, define	facts, stories, lists, definitions, formulas
Basic	2. Comprehension	understand, describe, restate, explain, summarize, identify	diagrams, puzzles, stories, reports, word problems
Somewhat complex	3. Application	use, perform, apply, solve, demonstrate, construct	maps, models, formulas, art, word problems, dialogues
Complex	4. Analysis	take apart, classify, sort, categorize, compare, contrast	graphs, charts, surveys, stories, objects, models
More complex	5. Synthesis	create, compose, design, develop, combine, plan	stories, articles, poems, experiments, hypotheses
Very complex	6. Evaluation	judge, evaluate, rate, decide, assess, criticize, defend	polls, panels, letters, reviews, surveys, simulations

Bloom's taxonomy can be easily integrated with the types of learning strategies that students use. The knowledge and comprehension levels fit nicely into the more basic learning tasks discussed previously, whereas application, analysis, synthesis, and evaluation can be incorporated in the more complex learning tasks. For example, sometimes students do not use strategies that address higher level thinking skills that a given task requires. These students could benefit from elaboration strategies aimed at making the formula more meaningful so that they could use it at the application and synthesis levels. On the other hand, some students asked to evaluate—the highest level of Bloom's taxonomy—instead act as court reporters and write down someone else's opinion. These students turn a high-level task into a basic learning task—that of rote repetition.

Knowing the expected outcome of a task in the taxonomy also can be quite beneficial for the teacher. As the worksheet illustrates, each level has key words that may make the directions clearer. For example, in the application stage, the student would be expected to use or demonstrate whatever content was learned. It helps to have in mind a clear goal of what you expect students to do in order to design tasks to meet these goals. Then you can explain the goals clearly to the students.

This may also be a good time to use any collaborative or cooperative groups you have set up. Each group might be responsible for determining the nature of the task and the expected outcome. You could exert some control as the teacher and make sure your own goals and objectives are met by specifying which level of Bloom's taxonomy should be addressed. For example, if you are discussing Texas history, you might give your groups the assignment of looking at how the Spanish influenced the lives of the native people living in what is now Texas. You could encourage your groups to be creative and give them a few guidelines. For example, they must produce a product that can be graded. The outcome should focus on synthesis and analysis of the facts. The students must work on the product as a group. They have 5 hours to complete the project (1 hour a day for a week) plus any outside time they might put into it.

If you have a younger group of students, or if this responsibility is new for your class, you might get them started by offering suggestions. For example, one group may decide to do a detailed map of what happened to the territory of the native people when the Spanish came. Another group may want to do a short play about how it affected specific historical figures of the period. Still another group could do a display of new art, tools, and food that came about when the cultures merged. All groups are using organizational and elaboration learning strategies to deepen and consolidate their understanding. For example, the cartography group is taking the general information of Spain's move into Texas and generating a detailed analysis of how it affected the population. The dramatic-interpretation group is taking the basic facts and synthesizing them into a short-story or play format. This can also be a motivating activity that would work with a whole class, with the teacher facilitating the discussion of what activity the class should choose. Having the learners take responsibility for their own learning is an important part of strategic learning.

Content Knowledge

It is important to help students understand that people remember things that are meaningful to them. A useful exercise may be to draw a long line on the chalkboard. Label one end *a few seconds,* and label the other end *forever.* Then fill in this line by asking your students what they remember only for a second. One student may say something like "my homework assignment for the next day!" This can be a fun activity. Other examples include a phone number or a new name. At the other end, they are likely to say they will always remember their name, their birthday, how to add 1-digit numbers, how to write the alphabet, or how to read. Then have them work into the middle. How long will they remember their vocabulary words? How long will they remember what they ate for lunch today? How long will they remember the order of the colors of the rainbow? Once the board is fairly full, have them discuss what qualities make people remember things longer. It should be fairly clear that people best remember things that are meaningful or personal to them. Using learning strategies helps people to make new information more meaningful so that it can become part of their knowledge. If you prefer to have them do this activity individually, a worksheet has been provided.

My Personal Memory Continuum

Name_____ Date _____

Instructions: Fill in the blanks with your own examples that range from things you don't remember very long (at the top of the page) to things you will remember a very long time (at the bottom of the page).

A few seconds   /   Page number of math homework_____

                     /   _____

                     /   _____

                     /   _____

                     /   _____

                     /   _____

                     /   Best friend's phone number_____

                     /   _____

                     /   _____

                     /   _____

                     /   _____

                     /   _____

                     /   _____

                     /   My home phone number_____

                     /   _____

                     /   _____

                     /   _____

                     /   _____

                     /   _____

Forever   /   My own name_____

Now try to extend how the memory continuum affects children's school learning. Ask your students if they have ever taken a test and thought they knew the material but couldn't remember it. Ask them how long they should be expected to know something. Ask them how difficult it is for them to remember their name. Compare that with learning a list of spelling words. Because it is fairly simple to remember things that are important or meaningful, the trick is to make school information meaningful.

It might be helpful at this point to give a fairly simplistic model of how the human brain works. You can ask how many of your students have a younger sibling or can remember listening to a toddler learning to talk. When a child first learns to talk, he or she tends to have very few labels under which to classify things. For example, every animal they see may be called a *dog*. After all, most animals that they see have four legs and a tail. Pretty soon they are able to distinguish between a dog and a cat. A cat is fluffier and usually smaller; a dog barks and a cat meows. So now the child has expanded on his or her categories and labels. There is an overarching *animal* label, and under that are the subcategories of *dog* and *cat*. It is even easier to remember this if the child has personal experience with the animal. For example, if the child was ever bitten by a dog, he or she is unlikely to forget that; in fact, it may color his or her perception of dogs even into adulthood. This is in part because the most important label people have is the one titled *me*. Anything people can connect to *me* becomes more meaningful and more likely to be remembered. The more links (or bridges) a concept has to *me* and to other categories and labels that have already been established, the more likely it is to be put into long-term storage. You can use an analogy of a maze of boxes to help your students envision this concept: Each box has its own label (*dog, cat, me*), and there are connections between each of the boxes. Emphasize that the more connections any box has to other boxes—especially the *me* box—the easier it is to remember the contents of that box. Each connection acts as a reminder, or a little flag, saying, "This way to the box you want." Students could be shown how useful it is to have these flags, particularly during test-taking time. It may also be helpful to show the sample-schema diagram that follows and ask students to complete their own.

Name: _____ Date: _____

Instructions: Fill out the following worksheet, thinking of two different things you know about. You may draw more circles if you need to, and you may change the connecting lines to best fit your own schemas.

Sample Schema

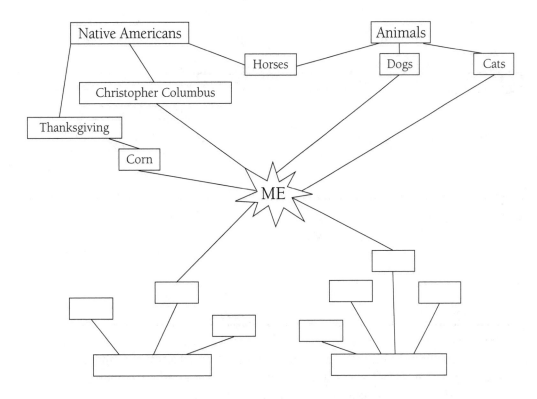

Think of a specific example you could use from your own class to illustrate the concept of bridges between boxes—linking prior knowledge to new knowledge. How would you teach the concept of memory? What flags would you use to cue your students to their prior knowledge boxes? How will you know the connection has been made?

1 Describe the lesson.

2 What flags or cues will you use?

3 How will you check your students' comprehension?

For the teacher, the task becomes identifying which children already have the appropriate prior knowledge and which children do not. Often, placement tests will give the teacher some information, but not everything taught is covered on the tests. In a way, the teacher becomes a sleuth, ferreting out which children need more background information before new information can be taught. You may need to look for clues that will help you solve this mystery. The following activity can help.

1 Which students do I suspect of needing more prior knowledge before I can go on to the next concept?

2 What clues will I look for to give me information?

3 How will I know or measure that the student has enough prior knowledge to move on?

4 How do I plan to remediate deficits?

5 Will I remediate individually or do so in groups? Why?

Context Knowledge

The following scenario discusses many aspects of context, the last area or domain of the skill component.

| STUDENT EXAMPLE: FRANKIE | Frankie is a seventh-grade boy in Mr. Brown's fifth-period English class. In this particular intermediate school, there are 20 minutes of class, then the students go to lunch, then there are another 30 minutes of class in fifth period. Frankie is into athletics and has a lot of energy (he has been tested for attention deficit disorder, and the doctor has prescribed Ritalin, but his parents don't want him to take it). He is usually hyperactive before lunch but extremely tired after it. He participates in athletics after school, and both of his parents work, so he doesn't go home until dinner time. After dinner, he usually watches some television, plays with his younger brother, gets ready for bed, and then does whatever homework he has. Mr. Brown is concerned because Frankie's grades are below what he believes his student's ability to be. He has discussed this with Frankie's parents, but they seem to be at a loss for how to help him improve his grades.

List as many of the contextual variables as you can find in the Frankie scenario.

1.

2.

3.

4.

Brainstorm some different strategies that could be used to help Frankie in school.

1.

2.

3.

4.

There are a lot of different contextual variables at work in this scenario. One of these is the context of the class; it is in the middle of the day, and the period is split, which may be distracting for the students and seems to be particularly distracting for Frankie. It is unclear from the scenario what is causing Frankie's mood swings, but the split period is an important variable to investigate. His motivation toward school is also unclear, though it appears that athletics are important to him. The scenario describes quite a bit about his home environment, and it could imply that he is not choosing the best time of the day to study.

From all of this information, teachers could generate some strategies for addressing some of the contextual factors that might be interfering with Frankie's ability to learn. For instance, it would be reasonable to check with Frankie's other teachers to see if he is experiencing a similar problem in their classes. If he is, then a team approach may be in order. If he is only having a problem in Mr. Brown's class, then Mr. Brown may want to investigate what learning or motivational issues need to be addressed. It would also be a fairly simple matter to talk with Frankie's parents about changing his study time to one that is more productive—perhaps between athletics and dinner time or right after dinner. Mr. Brown could also investigate Frankie's prior knowledge and see if there is a discrepancy or a large gap between what he already knows and the subject matter being taught.

It is important to remember that Frankie also should be taking some responsibility for his actions. As students go through their school careers, it is expected that they will take more and more responsibility for their actions and performance. Mr. Brown could ask Frankie, in a private setting because this is an individual problem, to help him analyze the discrepancy between his expectations for Frankie and Frankie's performance. Mr. Brown could encourage Frankie to set expectations for himself and come up with a plan for meeting those expectations. They could come up with a variety of strategies aimed at this end and some plan for implementation of these strategies. A way of getting feedback on Frankie's progress to the goals that he set for himself could be built into this plan. It is important for older students to begin setting their own learning goals because this is much more motivating than externally given goals.

Strategy Knowledge

Becoming More Fluent and Flexible

When it comes to strategy knowledge, fluency and flexibility are extremely important concepts for both teachers and students to grasp. *Fluency* refers to the number of strategies that the learner has at hand. Imagine if Frankie's teachers were asked to brainstorm about learning strategies. Some people would think of only one or two strategies. Some would be able to fill up a whole page. Those who could come up with a page full of strategies would be fluent but not necessarily flexible. *Flexibility* deals with the range, or different categories, of strategies used. If every strategy on the page dealt with different ways to positively reinforce Frankie for staying in his seat—check marks for good behavior, calling his parents when he had a good day, letting him skip one homework assignment if he worked quietly—this would not evidence flexibility. Flexible strategies would deal with Frankie staying in his seat, but they would also address other issues that were previously mentioned such as mood swings.

If a student is having difficulty with learning the material (or learning it to the level required), then it may be useful to work individually with that student to improve his or her strategy usage. There is never one perfect strategy that will solve all students' problems. Often, when it comes to learning and studying, students have a limited range of strategies from which to choose. However, teaching fluency and flexibility also can easily be done in small groups or with the whole class.

Small, collaborative groups could each be given one strategy to use to learn a particular content area. For instance, while learning a concept from a social studies text, one group might be told to use (or taught to use) outlining. One group might be told or taught to use imagery. One group might be told to teach it to someone. Then the groups could report back to the whole class about how that strategy worked with that particular task.

The same concepts of fluency and flexibility apply to different levels of learning and study strategies. For example, if the task being learned is more basic, such as learning multiplication tables, it may be useful to go over rehearsal strategies with the entire class. They could brainstorm ways of remembering lists. Here, it may be helpful for the teacher to model different ways of rehearsing. For example, you may want to show how a student could make his or her own flash cards. Using an organizational strategy along with rehearsal, you could show them how to memorize one list at a time (for example, they could memorize the entire 3s list—$3 \times 1 = 3$; $3 \times 2 = 6$, etc.—and look for patterns in that list). They could make a chart and cover the answer and repeat the list. This is also a good example of the impact of guided practice and feedback.

Teachers use guided feedback in many settings, which is important. Teachers wouldn't expect a third grader to go home with the assignment of memorizing all of the multiplication tables from 1 to 10 and then come in the next day and say them all. Instead, they assign small parts and give students feedback on their progress. Often this is done with a chart for each student that represents how far they have come in learning the entire table. Although guided practice with feedback is a familiar concept and is often used when teaching course content, it is important to remember that it is equally important when teaching learning skills.

It is important to reiterate that not every strategy works well for every task. Outlining may be useful in organizing and learning complex reading material, but it may not be as useful in understanding poetry. Strategic learners have a broad repertoire of strategies, so they have several choices of strategies to use with any one task. In this way, they are likely to be more efficient and effective.

Effectiveness and Efficiency in Strategy Use

Strategic learners know how to balance doing a good job and doing it in a reasonable amount of time. Students who are not as strategic tend to be too much on one side or the other. It is common to see a student who "miraculously" finishes his or her homework in 10 minutes. This student is truly efficient. Everything is done in a short time. Unfortunately, it is often done poorly. If this student does not learn better balance, he or she may be on the way to future academic difficulties. A less common though equally troubling pattern is the student who turns in beautiful work but labors much longer and harder than most of his or her classmates even though ability is not an issue. This student is effective but amazingly inefficient. A continuing pattern like this may lead to poor performance because the student will not be able to complete all of the work assigned and to high anxiety about schoolwork, particularly as the student advances in grades and the workload increases. Clearly, it is important for students to achieve a good balance of effectiveness and efficiency during their early school years.

If the content is more complex, say reading a story, you might ask the students to generate their own list of learning strategies aimed at upper level thinking (you might let them have a worksheet or chart of a sample of these strategies). Once they have chosen a strategy—and, in doing so, taken more responsibility for their learning—you could monitor their progress and give them feedback not only on how well they answer questions pertaining to the story but also on how well they implemented their strategy. Students could even keep a journal describing their experiences. If a student chose paraphrasing as an elaboration strategy, you could check the paraphrasing itself. Is it accurate? Does it include the main idea and important details? Is it too broad or too narrow in scope? It is only through practice in using new strategies and feedback on their success in using them that students will become more fluent and flexible in strategy choice, which will eventually lead to improved efficiency and effectiveness.

Think about students in your own class. How could you use the concepts of fluency and flexibility to improve their repertoire of learning and study skills?

1 For simple tasks (knowledge acquisition and comprehension):

2 For complex tasks (application, analysis, synthesis, evaluation):

We previously stated that strategic learners are aware of how they acquire knowledge. To do this both effectively and efficiently, strategic learners are fluent and flexible in their strategy knowledge and use; they know about and understand how to use learning strategies from a variety of different categories. They are aware of lots of different types of strategies that are available for different tasks. How do students become aware of all of these strategies? Often, this is done through modeling—both by the teacher and by the students' peers. For example, students often learn to take notes by copying down what the teacher writes on the board or the overhead projector. To help students develop more flexibility, teachers must model a wide variety of strategies for taking notes and use guided practice with feedback techniques to ensure that students have the opportunity to implement and refine their use of these strategies.

Teachers need to be aware of the different strategies, so we can help our students develop a useful repertoire of learning strategies. Many students do not develop a repertoire of effective and efficient strategies to help them successfully accomplish common school tasks. Even at the college level it is easy to find students relying heavily on simple memorization strategies (Weinstein & Meyer, 1991). These are the strategies with which they are most familiar, and because these methods are fairly labor-intensive (e.g., making note cards or taking notes verbatim), the students often feel that they are studying hard. In fact, they are. But studying hard is not the same thing as studying smart (Weinstein, 1992). These students at the college level, as well as students at the elementary, middle or junior high, and high school levels, would spend their time much more wisely by using learning strategies that fit with their personal characteristics, the task requirements, and their learning goals.

The following list of questions can be used to help students think about learning strategies aimed at higher level thinking and might encourage students to be more thoughtful about what "studying smart" really means. These questions can also be used by students on their own, to help them think about diverse learning strategies to help them reach their achievement goals.

Questions and Activities for Students That Teachers Can Use to Promote Higher Level Thinking

1. How could you use this in the project you are working on?
2. What is the moral of the story?
3. How is this formula like the one we just learned? How is it different?
4. What does this make you think about?
5. What does this remind you of?
6. What is the opposite of this idea?
7. What is the most important idea? What are three details about that idea?
8. What pictures does this make you think about?
9. How would you define this topic if you couldn't use a dictionary?
10. How would you teach this to your best friend?
11. How would you teach this to your parents?
12. How would you put this into your own words?
13. How could this idea be useful?
14. How could this concept be improved?
15. Draw a picture of this idea.
16. Make up a story using this idea.
17. What is the lesson to be learned from this?
18. What else do you need to find out in order to understand this concept?
19. What are the five most important points about this concept?
20. Compare and contrast this concept with the one we just learned.

Think of some questions, adapted either from the list just presented or your own experiences, that you could use to prompt the students in your own class to be more fluent and flexible. Use the following categories to classify them.

1 Rehearsal strategies

2 Elaboration strategies

3 Organization strategies

Everyone has strategies that she or he has used and improved over the years. These preferences are usually sufficient for peoples' learning needs. But what happens when a problem arises and preferred strategies do not work? If a person does not have a repertoire of diverse strategies, he or she will have no tools to fall back on in order to succeed. It is also important for students to use a systematic approach to learning and studying so that they can mindfully explore, develop, and refine their preferences. In Goal 4 we continue our discussion about the teaching of learning and study strategies, but the emphasis shifts to helping students develop a diverse repertoire of strategies.

SUGGESTED READINGS

Gagne, E. D. (1985). *The cognitive psychology of school learning.* Boston: Little, Brown.

Pressley, M., & Associates. (1993). *Cognitive strategy instruction that really improves children's academic performance.* Cambridge, MA: Brookline Books.

Weinstein, C. E., & McCombs, B. L. (Eds.). (in press). *Strategic learning: The merging of skill, will and self-regulation in academic context.* Hillsdale, NJ: Erlbaum.

goal 4

Helping Students Develop
a Repertoire of Strategies

To help students become more strategic learners, teachers need to know what students know, and students need to know what they know. Students bring a lot of perceptions and ideas about study and learning strategies with them when they come to school. Being able to assess students' existing knowledge about and use of learning strategies will help you target your efforts to their needs. Although there is no way to exhaustively evaluate students' knowledge and use of learning strategies, there are several ways you can get a good idea of their needs. This goal begins with a brief review of three assessment tools. Next, we review the importance of taking a strategic approach to learning. We provide an in-depth outline for teachers to follow when assigning a project to facilitate strategy use. Two student examples describe how different strategic learners faced the same task. These extended examples will increase your awareness of the possible variables that can affect the outcome of a learning task. Finally, we check back in with these students.

ASSESSING STUDENTS' LEARNING STRATEGIES

Talk Alouds

One way you can learn about the methods students use to learn different school tasks is to have them talk out loud while they are performing a task. For example, if a student is working on a puzzle, you could ask the student to say out loud what he or she is thinking as he or she tries to do it. It helps to model this procedure with an unrelated task and to give the student an opportunity to practice the talk-aloud procedure (Hume & Weinstein, 1994). It is a simple way to open a window on the mind and has been used successfully with many different academic tasks across the age span (Pressley & Afflerbach, 1995).

Probes

The use of probes to gather information about students' use of learning strategies has a long history. Real or imaginary learning tasks are presented to students, and they are asked (*probed*) directly about how they would go about learning the material. This can be done in an individual or a group setting (where students often learn from hearing the responses of their peers; Hume & Weinstein, 1994).

Self-Report Measures

A number of self-report measures are available for screening students' knowledge about or use of learning strategies. Although most of these are designed for college or high school students, the Learning and Study Strategies Inventory—High School Version (LASSI–HS; Weinstein & Palmer, 1990) also has been used successfully with 6th-, 7th-, and 8th-grade students. The LASSI–HS is a 76-item self-report instrument that assesses domains from all three components of strategic learning—skill, will, and self-regulation. The focus is on student thought processes and behaviors that impact studying and learning and that can be altered through educational interventions. There are 10 individual scales on the LASSI–HS: Attitude, Motivation, Time Management, Anxiety, Concentration, Information Processing, Selecting Main Ideas, Study Aids, Self-Testing, and Test Strategies. The scales that focus on the skill components of strategic learning are the Concentration, Information Processing, Selecting Main Ideas, Study Aids, and Test Strategies scales. Students receive feedback on each of the scales indicating where their strengths and weaknesses are in the different categories of strategic learning. Norms are provided for 9th-, 10th-, 11th-, and 12th-grade students, but the measure also has been used extensively with junior high school students and 6th graders.

A SYSTEMATIC APPROACH TO LEARNING

The two key components of self-regulation are awareness and control. *Control* deals with checking understanding, sometimes referred to as *comprehension monitoring*. It is not enough to simply try to learn the material. It is important to check to make sure that the information was learned correctly. How is this done? Basically, the strategies that were previously mentioned under acquiring knowledge also work for comprehension monitoring. So what is the essential difference? The difference is in the intent. For example, Shawna might use the strategy of paraphrasing the material to help herself learn it. However, unless she uses a comprehension-monitoring strategy, she will not be sure that she paraphrased correctly or has met the task requirements. So in order to check her understanding, she might use the strategy of teaching it to a classmate. If she has trouble explaining it or her classmate points out problems with her explanation, Shawna would see that she did not really understand the material.

The following two worksheets are designed to be templates for you and your students. The first worksheet can be used for you to generate pre-, during-, and poststrategies that might be appropriate for different tasks in your content area and grade level. This could then be duplicated for your students. The second worksheet is a template that your students can use to make conscious decisions about which strategies they would like to use before, during, and after an assignment. They can refer to your list as a starting place, but because the number of strategies that can be used for learning is large, students should be allowed and encouraged to develop strategies on their own. This is particularly important for older students in the upper elementary and junior high school grades. Once students complete it, the list becomes a tool for them to work from and a tool for you to give them feedback about their process of learning the material. It is also an excellent way for you to check their comprehension. If a student does not do well on the next quiz, you can use this worksheet to retrace his or her steps and find out where he or she went wrong. Because of this, you may want to suggest that students use at least one of the during strategies and one of the poststrategies that have some type of physical product, such as a picture if the student is using imagery or a paragraph if the student is summarizing or paraphrasing. It will be easier for the teacher and the student to find out what went wrong and then correct the problem.

Teachers of very young students will need to adapt this exercise even more. In the case of students at the kindergarten, first-grade, and second-grade levels, the teacher will need to be more directive. In other words, it is up to you to make the choices of pre-, during, and poststrategies for the students. Of course, as you begin to know your students better, you may find that they are able to choose between two alternatives. For example, you might give them a choice of learning the letter *B* by working with a partner and talking about all of the words they can think of that begin with that letter. Alternately, they might want to individually look at a picture and point out the objects that begin with the letter *B*. Because the acquisition of learning skills develops over time, it is up to you to judge how much responsibility you can transfer to your students. Part of this will depend on their prior knowledge. When students at any grade level are learning new strategies, they will not be able to make sound judgments about which strategies to use for which tasks. You will have to model how to make these judgments. As they gain expertise and increase their fluency and flexibility, they will be better able to make good, informed judgments. This rule applies even with older students. If they are not flexible (i.e., they don't have a large repertoire of strategies) or you are asking them to experiment with new strategies, you will need to be more directive as a teacher. It is only human for people to fall back on things with which they are comfortable. For example, it is common to see students at all levels using highlighters because it is a habit, even if it does not fit the task requirements well. If you would like your students to outline or diagram instead, you may need to limit their choice of strategies until they feel comfortable with the new strategies and are likely to use them on their own.

As we have illustrated in many examples, it is important to make strategy instruction explicit. Although it is not necessary to make an announcement every time you model a strategy, it is crucial that students are aware that they are active participants in the learning process who will increasingly have to make their own decisions about strategy selection and implementation. Strategic learners are aware that their choice of strategy influences their learning, so they try to choose wisely. You need to stress to your students that they can improve their learning by becoming more fluent and flexible, by learning more about themselves as learners, by being clear on what a task requires, and by knowing about and using available resources. They also need to develop a repertoire of learning strategies. If one strategy doesn't work, then it is important to have a fluent and flexible repertoire so that another one can be chosen.

Students' List of Possible Pre-, During, and Poststrategies

Name _____   Date _____

Assignment (What am I supposed to do?):

_____

_____

_____

_____

_____

_____

_____

_____

_____

_____

_____

Prestrategies   1. _____

                       2. _____

During strategies   1. _____

                       2. _____

                       3. _____

Poststrategies   1. _____

                       2. _____

STRATEGIC PLANNING: A PROJECT TO FACILITATE SYSTEMATIC STRATEGY USE

In order to help students become more systematic learners, it is helpful to take them through a systematic process designed to increase the fluency and flexibility of their strategy use. The following method is one that can be adapted to different content areas and grade levels.

| **A PROJECT TO FACILITATE SYSTEMATIC STRATEGY USE: TEACHER'S OUTLINE** | I. Define the Task: Decide What the Specific Task Requirements Are |

This information should be given very explicitly to the students.

> *EXAMPLE:* Mr. Valenzuela decides to assign a book report for his fifth-grade Texas history class. It is to be on a book from an approved list of biographies that will be provided for the students. The report should be between four and five hand-written pages (single-spaced). He will be deducting points for spelling and grammar mistakes. The report should briefly summarize the book (Bloom's comprehension level). The end of the report should explain in the student's own words how this historical character influenced Texas's historical develop-ment. In other words, it should answer the question, why was this person important? This last section is aimed at the more complex thinking skill of evaluation. The students will have 2 weeks to read the book and turn in the report.

II. Set Goal for the Task

Goal setting is addressed more thoroughly in other books in this series (e.g., Ridley & Walther, 1995); however, it does have an important impact on how students choose and use learning strategies. It is important that students explicitly set goals for learning tasks. These goals need to be realistic, challeng-ing, and specific, so the student will know when they are achieved. Saying "I want to do well" is not a clear goal. Saying "I want to get at least a B on my book report" is better.

III. Brainstorm Possible Strategies

At this point, the students should brainstorm possible strategies for accomplish-ing the task in a way that will help them reach their goal. This can be done in several ways. It can be done with or without teacher assistance. It can be done for the entire task, or the task can be broken down into smaller segments. Students can brainstorm individually, in groups, or as a whole class. The amount of brainstorming will vary according to the age of the students and the scope of the task—the younger the students and the smaller the scope, the fewer the number of strategies required.

Brainstorming is a simple process of coming up with as many ideas as possible to solve a problem. In the context of learning, brainstorming involves generating strategies that will help accomplish a task. There are only a few guidelines for brainstorming. First, any idea is an acceptable idea; even seemingly silly ideas may be useful when combined with other ideas, and sometimes silly ideas lead to very creative strategies. Second, the more strategies brainstormed the better. This is one case in which quantity can lead to quality. After the obvious strategies are quickly stated, students often become more flexible and creative with their strategy choices.

> *Example:* Mr. Valenzuela instructs his class to break the book report into two parts. The first brainstorming session should be about reading the text. The second brainstorming session should be about writing the paper. He allows the students to work in small cooperative groups. He states that each group must generate at least 15 strategies for reading and 15 strategies for writing. He starts the whole class off with the first 5 under reading:
>
> Check out a book
> Look at the summary on the back cover
> Look through major headings and chapter titles
> Outline while reading
> Summarize each chapter
>
> He reminds his students that they are just coming up with a list of possible strategies. They won't use every one; however, the better the list, the more good strategies they will have to choose from and the better the end product will be. Mr. Valenzuela then monitors the groups as they brainstorm for the next 20 minutes. At the end of class he assigns the brainstorming as homework. Each student can take whatever the group has generated, but he or she must come to class the next day with a total of 15 strategies for reading and 15 strategies for writing.

IV. Choose Strategies

After the brainstorming activity is complete, the students are ready to choose which strategies they would like to use. Now it is best to do this on an individual basis (unless, of course, it is a group project and not an individual task). By choosing their own strategies, students will be able to tailor their strategic plan to fit with their own personal characteristics (their strengths and weaknesses, interests, etc.). The teacher may want to give the students guidelines for how many strategies are acceptable or feedback on the strategies they have chosen before the students start to implement their plans.

> *Example:* Mr. Valenzuela requested that the students first state their personal goal for the task and then choose five strategies from their brainstorm lists, write those strategies down, and explain why they had chosen those particular strategies—that is, why they thought these strategies would help them meet their goal for the task. He reviewed their plans and made comments on their papers, sometimes individually questioning why the students had chosen particular strategies. If the students didn't seem to understand the purpose of the assignment, he spoke with them individually and asked them to revise their plans. Finally, his whole class had an initial set of strategic plans.

V. Implement and Monitor Strategies

At this point, the students are ready to implement their strategies. It is important that they do this consciously so that they are able to tell if their strategies are working (Garner, 1987; Paris & Newman, 1990). One fairly easy way of doing this is for the students to keep a log on how their strategy implementation is working.

VI. Strategy Evaluation

During this phase, the students will evaluate their strategy usage at the same time they are monitoring it. For example, if a student had chosen to read two chapters every night, but for the first 3 nights had only read five pages, this strategy is not working well, and it is time for a modification. The student should explain both why the strategy is not working and what he will do to remedy the problem—modifying the old strategy or deleting the old strategy and coming up with a new one. For example, the student mentioned previously may not have read more because he is in the band and has practice after school. In this case, he might decide to read during the weekend and get it done.

> *Example:* Mr. Valenzuela requests that the students keep a journal about how their strategies are working. He checks

these journals every few days and gives the students feedback on how they are doing—that is, how well they seem to be monitoring their strategy usage, how well they are evaluating their strategies, and how good their modifications appear to be, based on the evidence of the journal. For this task, there are really two parts to this plan; the first is for reading the book, and the second is for writing the paper.

VII. Evaluating the Strategic Plan

The final step in this systematic learning process is evaluating the plan after receiving feedback on the task. Once the student has earned a grade on the task, he or she will be better able to assess if he or she met the goal and what further modifications need to be done for the next task. Although teachers can (and should, particularly initially) make this project explicit and even give feedback on each part of the process, strategic learners understand that this is a cyclical process and that all feedback leads to modification and improvement, so that they can become more efficient and more effective with each task they undertake. It is this last step that many students skip. That is unfortunate because this is the step that helps students build up an effective and efficient repertoire of systematic approaches to learning.

> *Example:* Mr. Valenzuela handed back the book reports to his students. Some students seemed pleased, and some students seemed somewhat disgruntled. To ensure that his students reflected on the strategic planning process, he requested that his students write a one-page evaluation of their process for reading the book and writing the paper. He wanted them to include what they thought worked well, what worked poorly, and what they would do differently next time.

VIII. A Note on Grades

This project can be assessed in several different ways. All of the process papers (the strategic plan, the journal, and the one-page evaluation) and the final product (the task) could be combined in a portfolio assessment. The teacher may decide not to assign a grade to the process, instead just giving written feedback and giving a grade to the product. The reverse could also be done—grading the process, but not the product. Both pieces could be assigned a grade with different weights given according to the emphasis of the instruction. For example, you may want to have a unit on brainstorming, in which case the brainstorming component might receive more weight. Because this systematic approach to learning will be new for most of your students, it is important to make it an explicit assignment, to give some kind of feedback (grades, verbal feedback, or written feedback), and to assign it more than once. It is only by using this process repeatedly that students will be able to adapt it to fit their own needs and become more strategic, systematic learners.

My Strategic Plan

Name _____   Date _____

I. TASK CHARACTERISTICS

What is the task? (book report, paper, homework, experiment)

How long do I have to do it?

How well do I have to know it? (Bloom's taxonomy)

What resources are available to me? (library, lab, computer, etc.)

What else do I know about the task?

II. MY GOALS FOR THE TASK

What grade do I want to make?

How can I use this information now or in the future?

My Strategic Plan

Name _____   Date _____

III. BRAINSTORMING

My list of possible strategies:

1.

2.

3.

4.

5.

6.

7.

8.

9.

10.

11.

11.

13.

14.

15.

My Strategic Plan

Name _____   Date _____

IV. STRATEGIC PLAN

What strategies will I use? (Be specific. Note how long and how often each strategy will be used. Think about when, where, what, with whom, and why.)

Strategy 1

Strategy 2

Strategy 3

Strategy 4

(use another page if necessary)

My Strategic Plan

Name _____   Date _____

V. IMPLEMENTING AND MONITORING STRATEGIES

Describe in detail how you are carrying out your strategies. Include such details as when, where, and how you are implementing each strategy.

_____

Day 1

_____

Day 2

_____

Day 3

_____

Day 4

_____

Day 5

_____

Day 6

_____

Day 7

_____

Day 8

_____

My Strategic Plan

Name _____   Date _____

VI. STRATEGY EVALUATION AND MODIFICATION

Evaluate the success of each strategy as you use it. Decide what modifications could be done to improve your strategic plan.

Strategy 1

    Evaluation:

    Modification:

Strategy 2

    Evaluation:

    Modification:

Strategy 3

Evaluation:

Modification:

Strategy 4

Evaluation:

Modification:

My Strategic Plan

Name _____   Date _____

VII. OVERALL EVALUATION OF STRATEGIC PLAN

My final grade was _____ .
I did / did not meet my goal. (circle one)

On the rest of this page, evaluate the following:
1. What strategies worked?

Why?

2. What strategies didn't work?

Why?

3. What would I do the same next time?

4. What would I do differently next time?

Although the previous exercise is more appropriate for older students, the basic concepts are also important to introduce to younger children. At its most basic level a strategic plan involves knowing what one is supposed to do, deciding how to do it, doing it, seeing how well one has done it, and fixing any problems that arise. These are important skills for both young children and older ones. Although in the earlier elementary grades teachers would not be able to use the worksheets (and even the older elementary grade teachers will need to make some adaptations, such as reducing the number of strategies while brainstorming and when choosing a strategic plan), it is helpful for students of all ages to be able to go through the entire process. For younger students, this could be done by the teacher using a talk-aloud process to model the strategic plan. In talk-aloud procedures, people make explicit what their thought processes are. When using talk-alouds for instructional purposes, you can prompt students to go through the strategic process and give guidance and feedback at each step.

| TEACHER EXAMPLE: MS. JOHANSEN | Ms. Johansen, a first-grade teacher, is going to read a story to her students. She tells her students that she wants them to listen carefully and be able to tell her what happened in the story when she finishes. (She has given them the task characteristics.) She then says that she wants everyone to answer every question correctly. (She sets the goal for them.) She asks her students how they might remember everything that is going on in the story so that they can answer the questions she will ask at the end. (She is prompting a brainstorming activity.) She listens carefully to their answers and suggests that the students choose a few of the strategies, such as listening carefully and trying to picture in their minds what is happening in the story. (She is forming their strategic plan for them.) While she is reading, she stops occasionally to check for comprehension. When students answer incorrectly, she reminds them of their strategic plan and asks if they were using the strategies. Occasionally, she will modify a strategy, such as having a child move closer if he or she is having difficulty paying attention. (She is monitoring and modifying their strategy usage.) At the end of the story, she asks questions about it. At the end of the questioning time, she has her students form a line and decide how well they think they understood the story, with *perfectly—I could answer any question you asked about it* standing up at the front of the room and *not very well—I couldn't answer any questions about the story* standing at the back of the room, with students ranging from one extreme to the other with some in the middle. Once the students have found their place in line, she asks them more questions about the story to give them feedback on how well they have monitored their comprehension. Occasionally, she moves a student from one place in line to another to give them a physical demonstration of how well they know the

material. She asks them to think about what they could do next time to move up the line to really knowing everything about the story, and she promises that they will do the same activity the next time they read a story. (This demonstrates the final evaluation stage, when students evaluate their strategic plan and make decisions about how to improve it for future use.)

Notice that in this example, the teacher is being quite directive about which strategies are chosen, how the students' strategy usage is monitored and modified, and how the students do a final evaluation. The lack of student autonomy in this example is perfectly acceptable, because younger students need a lot of direction in order to practice using both new strategies (such as picturing the story in their mind) and the strategic plan (definition of the task through final evaluation; Pressley & McCormick, 1995; Woolfolk, 1998).

OTHER RELATED VARIABLES THAT WILL AFFECT THE LEARNING AND PERFORMANCE OUTCOMES

Although this book focuses on the role of learning and study strategies in strategic learning, strategic learners also need to be aware of their motivation, their self-regulation or self-management, and the context in which they are learning (time constraints, available resources, etc.). These other areas are discussed in other books in this series (e.g., Zimmerman et al.,1996). Strategic learners use their knowledge of all of these variables in order to make effective and efficient strategy choices. As we discussed previously, not every strategy will work for every task. However, there is more to analyze in choosing a strategy than simple task characteristics. For example, what is the student's level of motivation? Are students interested in the task? How much time do they have? What resources are available—library, computer, parents, tutors, study halls? How will they be able to use this knowledge in the future? The next two scenarios describe two very different strategic learners faced with the same task.

| STUDENT EXAMPLE: RANDY | *Variables Affecting Randy's Plan* |

Randy has an art project due in Mr. Wright's class. He was assigned the project on Monday, and it is due the following Monday. Randy plays football and has a big game on Thursday. He also knows he is going to be out of town for the weekend, and he has a lot of homework in other classes. The art project is to make a poster collage of his life. He can use original drawings, pictures from magazines, or photographs. Randy lives with his dad and a younger brother. He can't remember seeing magazines around the house, and he doesn't think there are many photos either. He thinks that art is a stupid class; he took it only because it fit in as an elective with his schedule and some of his friends also were taking it. Although he doesn't enjoy the class, grades are important to him. He wants to make at least a B in the class, so he knows he has to turn in something that is at least decent. He is not too worried, because he knows from past experience that once he gets an idea, his product is usually pretty good, and he has all week to think of an idea.

Randy's Strategic Plan

Randy recognizes that he has some major time constraints. He goes home and asks his dad if they can come home Sunday by noon because of his art project. When his father agrees, he calls his friends who are also in the class and asks them to come over Sunday afternoon and bring any magazines or pictures they might have. During the week, he thinks of how he can make a creative collage about himself, and decides to use the theme of football because that is his major interest. During the week, he hunts around his room for football-related items. He finds an old jersey that is too small, a photograph and an article from the local paper about his team, and some awards. He gets poster paper and construction paper from the art class. Sunday afternoon his friends come over and they all work on their collages. One of his friends brings some *Sports Illustrated* magazines, and Randy cuts out pictures related to football. He cuts his poster board into a human shape and fits the jersey onto it. He then pins the pictures, photos, and articles onto the jersey. He makes a helmet out of another piece of poster board and tapes it to the body. He declares the collage done. His friends think it's pretty good. Actually, he decides that it wasn't as bad as he thought it would be because he really enjoyed looking for all of the football-related material. He turns in the collage and gets an A−. His teacher liked the idea but said the product was somewhat sloppy. Randy agreed but was pleased with the outcome.

STUDENT EXAMPLE: DENISE | *Variables Affecting Denise's Plan*

Denise really enjoyed her art class, but when Mr. Wright assigned the collage project, she felt her heart sink. She didn't like tasks that were so vague. Denise didn't think she was very creative, and she had no idea what to do for the collage. She drew well, and in fact considered herself to be artistic, but she had problems coming up with ideas. She knew that at her house she had a lot of materials she could use. Denise had been interested in art for a long time, and she had collected a lot of supplies over the years. In addition to art supplies, it seemed like her mother subscribed to a hundred magazines, so

Denise was sure she had adequate resources. Also, this was a good week for Denise—she didn't have much homework, and except for going to the junior varsity football game Thursday night and the high school game Friday night, she knew she had a free weekend. This was fortunate, for although Denise was artistic, she was also a perfectionist, so every art project she did seemed to take her much longer than anyone else in the class.

Denise's Strategic Plan

Denise thought long and hard Monday about how to do her collage. She asked Mr. Wright if she could see what last year's class had done to get ideas. Mr. Wright agreed because he was familiar with Denise's work and knew she wouldn't just copy whatever she saw. Then Denise talked with some friends in the class and finally with her mother when she got home from school. She decided to do a chronology of her life in time-line fashion. She would have background pictures and paraphernalia from the year represented. She decided she would not have enough room to do every year, so she chose to do every 3 years. She split the poster board in half and taped the two halves together to make one long line. She then divided the longer line into five sections (birth to 3, 3 to 6, 6 to 9, 9 to 12, and 12 to present). She dug into old trunks and got out pictures of herself growing up. She also found some decorating magazines from the period of each age group. She asked her mom and dad what songs were popular during each period. She found her old pacifier, a little doll, a Barbie dress, her favorite book in the fifth grade, and a ribbon she had won recently. All of this went meticulously onto the timeline in the appropriate place. She labored long and hard and was very pleased with her end product. She turned in the collage and was rewarded with an A + .

Although Randy and Denise are both strategic learners with the same task, they have different variables to work with, from personal characteristics to motivation. Because of this, they have different strategic plans. However, they both reach their goals. This is really the heart of being a strategic learner. It is essential to be aware of variables that will affect the outcome of the task and then be able to generate a plan to address those variables. The following list of some possible variables may be helpful in several different ways. It may help you, as a teacher, be more aware of some of the different reasons students may not be doing as well as you would like in your class. For older students, it may be helpful to give them this list to help them brainstorm strategies related to their strengths and weaknesses on these variables (Paris & Newman, 1990; Pressley & McCormick, 1995; Woolfolk, 1998). The more students are aware of these variables, the more likely they are to generate a useful strategic plan. Younger students might also benefit from their teachers verbally reminding them of some of these variables as they approach different tasks.

Partial List of Variables That Can Affect Strategic Learning

Name: _____   Date: _____

1. What do you know about yourself as a learner? What are your strengths and weaknesses? What is your best time of day to study?

2. What do you know about the task? What are the specific requirements? How are you going to be graded?

3. How fluent and flexible are you in your strategies? Do you have a lot of learning strategies or do you use the same few strategies all of the time?

4. How much time do you have for this project? What other things do you have to do that will take away from your time working on this task?

5. What kind of goal have you set for yourself?

6. Do you monitor your use of strategies? Do you change them if they are not working?

7. What is your motivation level relative to this task? Are you interested in it? Do you think you can use this information later? Do you feel capable of doing it?

8. What resources are available to you at home and at school?

9. What does the teacher expect of you? What do you expect of yourself?

10. Have you ever done anything like this before? What do you already know about the subject or task?

11. Do you often procrastinate?

12. Are you a perfectionist?

13. Are you usually faster or slower than other students in your class in this subject?

14. Do you know when you know something and know when you don't know it?

15. Is it easy or hard for you to remember information in this subject?

Another way to use this list of possible strategies is to play a game with your students, inserting different variables into a scenario and asking them to come up with a strategic plan to accommodate those variables. This would look similar to the Randy and Denise scenarios. For example, you could start by saying

> Susan has (use an example from your class) due in a week.
> She also has (give a few time constraints). She (give motivation
> level) this class. She knows that (give her available resources).
> She wants to make (give a goal of a specific grade) on this
> project. What can she do to meet her goal?

At this point, the students can brainstorm possible strategies, see how they fit with the characteristics you have given about Susan, and then make a strategic plan for her. This could lead to productive discussion about which strategies might address which variables. It would then be easy to pick another student's name and insert different variables.

CHECKING BACK WITH JULIET AND RAMON

In the introduction to this book, we introduced Juliet and Ramon. Based on the information about learning and study strategies we presented in the other chapters, examples of how a teacher might work with Juliet and Ramon to improve their success in school are presented here.

JULIET

Juliet's teacher is concerned that Juliet's reading difficulties will adversely affect her motivation to stay in school. As the teacher analyzes Juliet's difficulties, she notices that Juliet is able to perform tasks at a very low level of Bloom's taxonomy. She can repeat sentences and do very simple recognition tasks, but she is lost when the task requires higher level thinking.

Juliet's teacher makes a strategic plan to slowly foster her higher level thinking skills. Because Juliet appears to be unable to string the individual sentences together in order to generate meaning from them, her teacher decides to alter the assignment for her. Before Juliet begins to read a story, her teacher gives her a brief summary of it. The teacher then shows her the questions she will need to answer after she reads. Juliet is asked to paraphrase each sentence as she reads it and write it down to the side. Then after each paragraph, she is to paraphrase the paragraph. When she thinks she can answer one of the questions, she is told to do so and read back in the story to make sure she has answered the question correctly. At the end of the story she is asked to paraphrase the entire story and see how close she came to the original summary she heard. Then she is to attempt to answer any questions that are remaining.

Juliet's teacher realizes that this new method is time-consuming, so she limits the quantity of reading that Juliet is to do. She also encourages Juliet's progress and, initially, spends quite a bit of time with her individually. Eventually, Juliet is allowed to summarize just the paragraphs instead of each sentence. Finally, Juliet is almost on par with the rest of the class in her reading ability. Juliet's teacher feels that her strategic plan for Juliet has been a success.

RAMON

Ramon's homeroom teacher, Mr. Garrison, decides to hold a conference with all of Ramon's teachers. It seems to all of them that Ramon is working hard but is not getting the results he would like. Mr. Garrison suggests that the teachers come up with a strategic plan for Ramon to get him on the right track. They brainstorm different possibilities and decide that part of Ramon's problem is that he doesn't completely understand many task characteristics. Each teacher plans to be more explicit when giving their instructions. Next, they plan to involve

Ramon in making his own strategic plan for studying. Each teacher will check Ramon's study plan to see if it matches the task requirements. Then they will help Ramon with his comprehension monitoring. Before a test, they will give him a miniquiz, to see if he understands the material. If he doesn't, they will look back at his strategic plan and see what needs to be corrected.

Two teachers complain that this will be time-consuming and seems to give Ramon an unfair advantage. Mr. Garrison counters that currently Ramon seems to be struggling with an unfair disadvantage—he is working hard, but he is not working smart. Mr. Garrison also notes that the monitoring and the prequizzing should be done by Ramon himself as soon as he has become a more strategic learner. In fact, it wouldn't hurt the rest of the class to strategically plan and prequiz also; thus, Ramon wouldn't need to take up inordinate amounts of the teacher's time. Finally, Mr. Garrison points out that by involving all of his teachers, and by calling his parents and involving them also, Ramon should become a strategic learner much more quickly because his learning-strategies development would be reinforced in every class and at home.

He ends the meeting by saying, "And remember, this is only one strategic plan. If it doesn't work, we shouldn't give up on Ramon. We will just come back and meet again and decide what actions need to be revised, thrown away, or added." The teachers leave the meeting with hope for Ramon and with ideas for the rest of their students as well.

SUGGESTED READINGS

Pintrich, P. R., & Schunk, D. H. (1996). *Motivation in education: Theory, research, and applications.* Englewood Cliffs, NJ: Simon & Schuster.

Pressley, M., & McCormick, C. B. (1995). *Advanced educational psychology: For educators, researchers, and policymakers.* New York: HarperCollins.

Schunk, D. H. (1996). *Learning theories* (2nd ed.). Englewood Cliffs, NJ: Prentice Hall.

final review

As teachers, there are many skills and large amounts of information, ideas, concepts, and principles we want our students to learn. Good teaching involves all of these things, but it also involves a negotiation and transfer of the responsibility for learning from the teacher to the student. An educated person knows about science, but he or she also knows how to learn more about science and how scientists think about their world. Teachers all need to teach today's knowledge and skills, but we must help our students develop the learning strategies they will need to learn tomorrow's knowledge also.

The following list is a summary of the main ideas and concepts presented in this text.

☐ Students are active learners who construct, integrate, reorganize, modify, and add to their various knowledge bases. However, many students are not strategic in their approach to learning and studying.

☐ Cognitive, behavioral, motivational, affective, and self-regulated learning and study strategies can be modified by educational interventions. Teachers need to provide more systematic instruction in learning strategies so that students can explore and discover the methods that work best for them to meet various learning demands and goals. Students need to become aware of the many and different ways that they can process information. They must learn how to evaluate the effectiveness of different strategies for different learning situations, goals, and contexts. Strategic learners know how to make choices about how to learn and have a repertoire of strategies that they can select from to implement these choices.

☐ Strategic learners are aware of personal characteristics that can impact the difficulty or ease of learning.

☐ Strategic learners know about the nature of academic tasks and the types of strategies that will help them accomplish different tasks.

☐ Strategic learners build bridges between what they already know and what they are trying to learn.

☐ Strategic learners are aware of the context in which they are learning and how that context frames, constrains, and supports studying and learning.

☐ There are three types of learning strategies: rehearsal, elaboration, and organizational strategies.

☐ Students need a repertoire of learning and study strategies so that they can develop their preferences for recurring tasks and meet the challenges of new or problematic learning situations.

☐ Rehearsal strategies focus on repetition to increase familiarity and memory. Rehearsal strategies for basic learning tasks focus on simple repetition to increase familiarity and memory. Rehearsal strategies for complex learning tasks focus on selection of important information and repetition to increase familiarity, understanding, and memory. Rehearsal strategies for complex learning tasks involve more active thinking on the part of the student.

☐ Elaboration strategies help students to build bridges between what they already know and what they are trying to learn and remember. By elaborating on or adding to the material, students build up meaning and help to move the new information along the memory continuum. Using these strategies also helps students to organize and integrate their new and old knowledge in meaningful ways. This not only helps to make the new information more understandable and memorable but also helps to generate a usable data base for higher order thinking and application.

☐ Organizational strategies focus on reducing the load on working memory and helping to build meaning for the new information students are trying to learn. Organizational strategies usually involve chunking things together into larger clusters or imposing a conceptual framework on a set of items.

☐ Using the different types of strategies (rehearsal, elaboration, and organization) requires three types of knowledge: declarative, procedural, and conditional knowledge. Declarative knowledge is what students need to know about different strategies and their characteristics. Once students know about strategies and their characteristics, it is important to quickly move on to teaching them how to use these strategies (procedural knowledge). As students gain expertise in using learning strategies, it is also important that they learn about the conditions under which it is or is not useful to use a particular strategy (conditional knowledge).

☐ Learning strategies can also be divided into pre-, during-, and posttask strategies. Prestrategies deal with preparation. During strategies deal directly with building meaning for knowledge acquisition, or how one actually learns the content. The last group of strategies are the poststrategies. These come after information has been put into memory locations. Here, the strategic learner goes back and looks to see if the information that was placed in the location was the right information and if it really belonged in the location in which it was initially placed. It is important to check one's comprehension after an attempt at acquiring new knowledge. Strategic learners take responsibility for this themselves.

☐ Strategic learners need to be both fluent and flexible in their strategy use. Fluency is to the number of strategies that the learner has at hand. Flexibility deals with the range, or different categories, of strategies students know about and can use.

□ Strategic learners know how to balance effectiveness and efficiency—doing a good job in a reasonable amount of time—in using strategies to meet their learning goals.

□ By integrating the teaching of learning and study strategies into the curriculum and classroom, teachers can have a tremendous impact on helping students to become strategic learners. This can be accomplished by providing specific opportunities for students to learn about strategies (direct instruction), modeling the use of strategies across task types and content areas (modeling), and providing guided practice and feedback for students as they acquire new strategies or deepen their understanding and use of existing strategies (guided practice with feedback). Usually, teachers will use some combination of these three general approaches to instruction.

□ Direct instruction involves telling students about the strategies and how to use them.

□ Modeling requires the teacher to demonstrate how to use the strategy.

□ Guided practice with feedback usually is used after direct instruction and modeling so that students can try out the strategies and get feedback about their choices and implementation. This usually is implemented over a prolonged period so that students get a chance to continue refining their procedural and conditional strategy knowledge. This also can help students to develop systematic approaches to studying and learning so that the use of learning and study strategies becomes more routinized and does not require excess thought that can distract students from the learning or studying task at hand. It is only through practice in using new strategies and feedback regarding their success in using them that students will become more fluent and flexible in strategy choice, which will eventually lead to improved efficiency and effectiveness.

□ Students bring a lot of perceptions and ideas about study and learning strategies with them when they come to school. It is helpful to assess students' existing knowledge about and use of learning strategies, so that teachers can target their efforts to student needs. One way teachers can learn about the methods students use to learn different school tasks is to have them talk out loud while they are performing a task. The use of probes to gather information about students' learning strategies also can be helpful. Real or imaginary learning tasks are presented to students, and they are asked (probed) directly about how they would go about learning the material. A number of self-report measures, such as the LASSI–HS, also are available for screening students' knowledge about or use of learning strategies.

By helping students to develop an effective and efficient repertoire of learning strategies that they can use as part of a strategic approach to studying and learning, teachers are helping them to develop skills and knowledge that they will need for lifelong learning.

glossary

at-risk students—students who may experience failure or low achievement. Can be due to a variety of reasons, including poor learning strategies.

chunking—combining things in memory into meaningful clusters so that individual items can be assessed more easily.

clustering—a process by which people arrange things they are trying to learn into categories to make them easier to learn.

cognition—the study of thoughts and thought processes and their relation to behaviors, emotions, and beliefs.

conditional strategy knowledge—knowledge about when it is and is not appropriate to use a particular strategy.

context variables—environmental variables that affect student learning, such as teacher expectations, classroom resources, and peer support.

declarative strategy knowledge—knowledge about strategies and their characteristics.

direct instruction—a portion of class time set aside to specifically teach students about learning strategies.

effective learner—a student who takes a systematic approach to studying and learning so that he or she is more likely to reach his or her learning goals and to accomplish this in an efficient manner (also see *strategic learners*).

effort or strategic effort—spending the time needed to reach learning goals (diligence) and being strategic about how to use that time.

elaboration strategies—learning strategies using what students already know to help build bridges to what they are trying to learn.

flexibility—the number of different individual strategies that people generate for learning something or solving a learning problem.

fluency—the number of different categories of strategies that people generate for learning something or solving a learning problem.

guided practice and feedback—a process by which students practice using learning strategies and receive feedback from the teacher about their choice and implementation of one or more strategies.

knowledge base—a student's existing knowledge.

learning and study strategies—thoughts, beliefs, and actions that facilitate and mediate acquiring, storing, and accessing knowledge. A method or approach that incorporates the steps needed to reach a learning goal.

modeling—learning strategies instruction where the teacher demonstrates how to use particular strategies.

organizational strategies—learning strategies that impose an organizational framework onto the information students are trying to learn to help make it more meaningful.

prior knowledge—existing knowledge that students can use to help to build meaning for what they are trying to learn.

procedural strategy knowledge—knowledge about how to use strategies.

rehearsal strategies—learning strategies using active, mindful repetition.

self-regulated learners—students who can select and manage their own learning and study strategies and who can monitor their progress toward learning goals.

strategic learners—students who view studying and learning as a systematic process that is, to a good degree, under their control.

strategy—a method or approach that incorporates the steps needed to reach a goal.

talk alouds—when the student or teacher says out loud what he or she is thinking.

working memory—that portion of memory where people process the information they are currently thinking about or trying to learn.

references

Alexander, P. A., & Judy, J. E. (1988). The interactions of domain-specific and strategic knowledge in academic performance. *Review of Educational Research, 58,* 375–404.

Ames, C., & Archer, J. (1988). Achievement goals in the classroom: Students' learning strategies and motivation processes. *Journal of Educational Psychology, 80,* 260–267.

Anderson, J. R. (1990). *Cognitive psychology and its implications* (3rd ed.). New York: Freeman.

Baddeley, A. D. (1992). Working memory. *Science, 255,* 556–559.

Basden, B. H., Basden, D. R., Devecchio, E., & Anders, J. A. (1991). A developmental comparison of the effectiveness of encoding tasks. *Genetic, Social, and General Psychology Monographs, 117,* 419–436.

Bloom, B. S. (1956). *Taxonomy of educational objectives: Cognitive domain.* New York: McKay.

Ericsson, K. A., & Polson, P. G. (1988). An experimental analysis of the mechanisms of a memory skill. *Journal of Experimental Psychology: Learning, Memory, and Cognition, 14,* 305–316.

Gagné, E. D. (1985). *The cognitive psychology of school learning.* Boston: Little, Brown.

Gall, M. D., Gall, J. P., Jacobsen, D. R., & Bullock, T. L. (1990). *Tools for learning.* Alexandria, VA: Association for Supervision and Curriculum Development.

Garner, R. (1987). *Metacognition and reading comprehension.* Norwood, NJ: Ablex.

Guthrie, J. T., Van Meter, P., McCann, A. D., Wigfield, A., Bennett, L., Poundstone, C. C., Rice, M. E., Faibisch, F. M., Hunt, B., & Mitchell, A. M. (1996). Growth of literacy engagement: Changes in motivations and strategies during concept-oriented reading instruction. *Reading Research Quarterly, 31,* 306–332.

Hume, L. M. & Weinstein, C. E. (1994). Talk-alouds: Windows on the mind. *Innovation Abstracts, 16*(16), 1–2.

Jones, B. F., & Idol, L. (Eds.). (1990). *Dimensions of thinking and cognitive instruction.* Hillsdale, NJ: Erlbaum.

Klatzky, R. L. (1980). *Human memory: Structures and processes* (2nd ed.). New York: Freeman.

Manning, B. H. (1995, April). *Translating self-regulated learning theory and research into classroom instruction.* Paper presented at the annual meeting of the American Educational Research Association, San Francisco.

Mayer, R. E. (1996). Learners as information processors: Legacies and limitations of educational psychology's second metaphor. *Educational Psychologist, 31*(3/4), 151–161.

McCombs, B. L. (1994). Strategies for assessing and enhancing motivation: Keys to promoting self-regulated learning and performance. In H. F. O'Neil, Jr., & M. Drillings (Eds.), *Motivation: Theory and research* (pp. 49–69). Hillsdale, NJ: Erlbaum.

McCombs, B. L., & Pope, J. E. (1994). *Motivating hard to reach students.* Washington, DC: American Psychological Association.

McKeachie, W. J. (1994). *Teaching tips.* Lexington, MA: Heath.

Miller, G. A. (1956). Magical number 7, plus or minus two: Some limits on our capacity for processing information. *Psychological Review, 63,* 81–97.

Paris, S. G., & Ayres, L. R. (1994). *Becoming reflective students and teachers with portfolios and authentic assessment.* Washington, DC: American Psychological Association.

Paris, S. G., Lipson, M. Y., & Wixson, K. K. (1983). Becoming a strategic reader. *Contemporary Educational Psychology, 8,* 293–316.

Paris, S. G., & Newman, R. S. (1990). Developmental aspects of self-regulated learning. *Educational Psychologist, 25,* 87–102.

Pintrich, P. R., & De Groot, E. V. (1990). Motivational and self-regulated learning components of classroom academic performance. *Journal of Educational Psychology, 82,* 33–40.

Pintrich, P. R., & Schunk, D. H. (1996). *Motivation in education: Theory, research, and applications.* Englewood Cliffs, NJ: Simon & Schuster.

Pressley, M., & Afflerbach, P. (1995). *Verbal protocols of reading.* Hillsdale, NJ: Erlbaum.

Pressley, M., & Associates (1993). *Cognitive strategy instruction that really improves children's academic performance.* Cambridge, MA: Brookline Books.

Pressley, M., Borkowski, J. G., & Schneider, W. (1987). Cognitive strategies: Good strategy users coordinate metacognition and knowledge. In R. Vasta & G. Whitehurst (Eds.), *Annals of child development* (Vol. 5; pp. 89–129). Greenwich, CT: JAI Press.

Pressley, M., & McCormick, C. B. (1995). *Advanced educational psychology: For educators, researchers, and policymakers.* New York: HarperCollins.

Puntambekar, S. (1995). Helping students learn "how to learn" from texts: Towards an ITS for developing metacognition. *Instructional Science, 23*(1–3), 163–182.

Ridley, D. S., & Walther, B. (1995). *Creating responsible learners: The role of a positive classroom environment.* Washington, DC: American Psychological Association.

Rosenshine, B. (1995). Advances in research on instruction. *Journal of Educational Research, 85*(5), 262–268.

Schunk, D. H. (1989). Social cognitive theory and self-regulated learning. In B. J. Zimmerman & D. H. Schunk (Eds.), *Self-regulated learning and academic achievement* (pp. 83–110). New York: Springer-Verlag.

Schunk, D. H. (1996). *Learning theories* (2nd ed.). Englewood Cliffs, NJ: Prentice Hall.

Schunk, D. H., & Zimmerman, B. J. (1997). Social origins of self-regulatory competence. *Educational Psychologist, 32,* 195–208.

Shapley, K. S. (1995, April). *Developing self-regulated learners in the middle school.* Paper presented at the annual meeting of the American Educational Research Association, San Francisco.

Sternberg, R. J., & Spear-Swerling, L. (1996). *Teaching for thinking.* Washington, DC: American Psychological Association.

Van Hout Wolters, B. (1994). Selecting and cueing key phrases in instructional texts. In H. Mandl, E. De Corte, N. Bennett, & H. F. Friedrich (Eds.), *Learning and instruction* (pp. 181–198) Frankfurt, Germany: Pergamon Press.

Weinstein, C. E. (1978). Teaching cognitive elaboration learning strategies. In H. F. O'Neil, Jr. (Ed.), *Learning strategies.* New York: Academic Press.

Weinstein, C. E. (1992). Working hard is not the same as working smart. *Innovation Abstracts, 14*(5), 1–2.

Weinstein, C. E. (1994). Strategic learning/strategic teaching: Flip sides of a coin. In P. R. Pintrich, D. R. Brown, & C. E. Weinstein (Eds.), *Student motivation, cognition, and learning: Essays in honor of Wilbert J. McKeachie* (pp. 257–273). Hillsdale, NJ: Erlbaum.

Weinstein, C. E., Husman, J., & Dierking, D. R. (in press). Strategic learning. In C. E. Weinstein & B. L. McCombs (Eds.), *Strategic learning: The merging of skill, will and self-regulation in academic contexts.* Hillsdale, NJ: Erlbaum.

Weinstein, C. E., & Mayer, R. E. (1986). The teaching of learning strategies. In M. C. Wittrock (Ed.), *Handbook of research on teaching* (3rd ed., pp. 315–327). New York: Macmillan.

Weinstein, C. E., & McCombs, B. L. (Eds.). (in press). *Strategic learning: The merging of skill, will and self-regulation in academic contexts.* Hillsdale, NJ: Erlbaum.

Weinstein, C. E., & Meyer, D. K. (1991). Cognitive learning strategies and college teaching. In R. J. Menges & M. E. Svinicki (Eds.), *College teaching: From theory to practice. New directions for teaching and learning* no. 45. San Francisco: Jossey-Bass.

Weinstein, C. E., & Palmer, D. R. (1990). *The Learning and Study Strategies Inventory—High School Version.* Clearwater, FL: H & H Publishing.

Wittrock, M. C. (1990). Generative processes of comprehension. *Educational Psychologist, 24,* 345–376.

Wittrock, M. C., & Alesandrini, K. (1990). Generation of summaries and analogies and analytic and holistic abilities. *American Educational Research Journal, 27*(3), 489–502.

Woolfolk, A. E. (1998). *Educational psychology* (7th ed.). Boston: Allyn & Bacon.

Zimmerman, B. J. (1989). A social cognitive view of self-regulated academic learning. *Journal of Educational Psychology, 81,* 329–339.

Zimmerman, B. J. (1990). Self-regulated learning and academic achievement [Special issue]. *Educational Psychologist, 25*(1).

Zimmerman, B. J., Bonner, S., & Kovach, R. (1996). *Developing self-regulated learners: Beyond achievement to self-efficacy.* Washington, DC: American Psychological Association.

ABOUT THE AUTHORS

Claire Ellen Weinstein, PhD, is a professor of educational psychology and chair of the concentration in learning, cognition, and instruction at the University of Texas at Austin. She has a doctorate in educational psychology from the University of Texas at Austin. She has 21 years of experience in research and development of learning and study-strategies interventions and assessment instruments for students, teachers, and parents. Her particular area of expertise is helping individuals to become more strategic, self-regulated learners who can play a more active role in and take more responsibility for their own studying and learning.

Laura M. Hume is a graduate student in the doctoral program in the Department of Educational Psychology at the University of Texas at Austin. She has a BS degree in curriculum, education, and instruction from Texas A&M University, College Station, Texas. She has taught 6th-, 7th-, 11th-, and 12th-grade English in the Texas public school system and is currently a staff-development specialist for Arthur Anderson and Associates.